Harvard Publications in Music

1. The Complete Works of Anthony Holborne, edited by Masakata Kanazawa. Volume I: Music for Lute and Bandora.
2. The Symphonies of G. B. Sammartini, edited by Bathia Churgin. Volume I: The Early Symphonies.
3–4. The Lute Music of Francesco Canova da Milano (1497–1543), edited by Arthur J. Ness. Volumes I and II (2 vols. in 1).
5. The Complete Works of Anthony Holborne, edited by Masakata Kanazawa. Volume II: Music for Cittern.
6. The Operas of Alessandro Scarlatti, Donald Jay Grout, General Editor. Volume I: Eraclea, edited by Donald Jay Grout.

Harvard Publications in Music, 6

THE OPERAS OF ALESSANDRO SCARLATTI
Donald Jay Grout, General Editor
Volume I

To my colleagues in the Music Department of
Cornell University

Acknowledgments

It is a pleasure to express my gratitude to institutions and individuals who have contributed to this edition of *Eraclea*. I wish to thank Cornell University for numerous faculty research grants and a favorable teaching schedule; my colleagues and students in the Department of Music for encouragement and practical assistance; the U.S. Department of State for a Fulbright-Hayes Research Grant to Belgium in 1965–66; Mrs. André de Flandre and the staff of the U.S. Educational Foundation in Brussels; and the National Endowment for the Humanities for substantial grants in 1968 and 1969–70.

To the following librarians and their staffs I am grateful for permission to make use of their holdings and for friendly assistance: Albert Vander Linden, Bibliothèque du Conservatoire Royal de Musique, Brussels; Bernard Huys, Music Section, Bibliothèque Royale, Brussels; Anna Mondolfi Bossarelli, Biblioteca del Conservatorio S. Pietro a Majella, Naples; Alexander Hyatt King and Pamela J. Willetts, The British Museum, London; Robert Latham, the Pepys Library, and the Master and Fellows of Magdalene College, Cambridge; Peter Riethus and the Music Division of the Osterreichische Nationalbibliothek, Vienna; Vladimir Fédorov and François Lesure, Music Department, Bibliothèque Nationale, Paris; Dr. Burgmeister, Director, and Dr. Reich, Head of the Music Division, Sächsische Landesbibliothek, Dresden; Napoleone Fanti and Giovanni Falzone, Civico Museo Bibliografico Musicale, Bologna; Marcello Paravani, Biblioteca del Conservatorio, Parma; Emilia Zanetti, Biblioteca S. Cecilia, Rome; Harald Heckmann, Deutsches Musikgeschichtliches Archiv, Kassel; H. J. Van Royen, Instituut voor Muziekwetenschap, Utrecht; and in particular, Claudio Sartori, Biblioteca Nazionale Braidense, Milan, for much valuable bibliographical information.

The following have kindly responded to inquiries and made valuable suggestions: Armen Carapetyan, Oliver Strunk, George J. Buelow, Owen Jander Daniel Heartz, Eduard Reeser, Sven Hansell, and William C. Holmes. I am particularly indebted to Robert A. Hall, Jr., for his translation of the libretto, and to Edwin Hanley and Michael Collins for information about many details of the scores and counsel in matters of transcription. Finally, I wish to express my appreciation to the Department of Music of Harvard University and to the Harvard University Press for undertaking the publication of *The Operas of Alessandro Scarlatti*, of which *Eraclea* constitutes the first volume.

"Cloudbank"
Skaneateles, New York

D.J.G.

Contents

Contents

INTRODUCTION

The Story of Eraclea

Like innumerable opera plots of the early eighteenth century, that of *Eraclea* takes as its starting point—one might rather say, its jumping-off place—an episode of ancient history. Heraclia (Eraclea) was a daughter of Hiero, King of Syracuse in Sicily, a steadfast friend and ally of Rome in the second Punic War. Hiero died at an advanced age in 215 B.C. and was succeeded by his grandson Hieronymous. This youth of fifteen was so hated, because of his haughty manners and because he was suspected of a design to betray Syracuse to the Carthaginians, that he was assassinated by his own followers after a reign of only thirteen months. Two of his guardians who were connected by marriage with the royal family then plotted to seize power but were detected and executed; the enraged magistrates further decreed that every surviving member of the royal house should be killed. Livy gives a most pathetic account of the slaughter by the soldiers of Heraclia and her two daughters—a deed rendered the more pitiful because, it was said, a messenger with an order countermanding the execution had arrived too late.[1]

Besides Heraclia, two other figures from Roman history appear in this opera: M. Claudius Marcellus (Marcello), a distinguished Roman consul and general who besieged and eventually captured Syracuse in 212 B.C. after the celebrated engines of Archimedes had enabled the city to hold him off for two years, and Decius Magius (Decio), an official of the city of Capua who had resisted the blandishments of Hannibal and had tried, though ineffectually, to hold his countrymen to their pledged alliance with Rome. "All this," remarks Stampiglia in his "Argomento" at the front of the libretto, "you will find plainly in Titus Livius. The remainder is invented."

The inventions, in fact, constitute practically the entire opera. Instead of being killed by the soldiers, Eraclea and her daughters are rescued—first by the intervention of Decio and his page Livio and then by the timely arrival of Damiro with the news of the repeal of the order for their death. Decio has come to Syracuse expressly to protect Eraclea, with whom he has fallen in love through having learned of her beauty and goodness from her late husband at Alexandria. (The voluntary exile, though not the early death, of Heraclia's husband is historical fact.) In order better to carry out his self-imposed mission, Decio has disguised himself as a woman under the name of Aldimira. Eraclea, who, it now appears, is the reigning monarch of Syracuse, responds to Decio's love, but their union is hindered by two circumstances. Marcello, arriving in all the glory of a conqueror, promptly falls in love with Eraclea; she feels constrained to placate him by avoiding an outright refusal of his suit for fear of possible consequences to her city,

1. Livy, *Historiae*, bk. XXIV, ch. xxvi.

herself, and her daughters. Decio, likewise, from loyalty to Rome and its representative, feels obliged to give up Eraclea to Marcello. This classic conflict between love and duty is resolved only in the final scene of the opera when Marcello, being apprised of the situation, magnanimously resigns all claim to Eraclea so that she may marry Decio.

Running alongside the central drama and intersecting it only incidentally are two other lines of action: a romantic comedy and a farce. Eraclea's daughters Flavia and Irene become involved in love affairs with Damiro and his friend Iliso. The couples quarrel, the girls exchange lovers and then regret it; more quarrels end at last with reconciliation and happy unions. The farcical element is provided by Decio's page, Livio, who, like his master, has arrived in woman's costume and who, under the name of Lilla, amuses himself by tempting Alfeo, tutor to Eraclea's daughters, a solemn conceited old pedant who has always prided himself on his stoic immunity to female charms. These scenes with Livio and Alfeo are among the best of their kind in all Scarlatti's operas; of course they have no bearing whatever on either of the other two plots, being inserted simply to provide occasional comic relief.

The following diagram shows how the three spheres of action alternate throughout the opera. The main plot occupies the salient positions: the beginning and ending of each act and the first scene after each change of stage set except for III.ii. The scenes of the romantic comedy are often systematically grouped, alternating the two pairs of lovers, and in some of these scenes the dialogue itself is cast in markedly symmetrical form.[2] The farcical interludes are spaced apart, each usually following, and in one instance (III.ii) parodying, a scene of action relating to the central drama. Connections among the three groups of personages appear only sporadically except at the beginning of Act I and in the final scene of Act III.

	The Drama	The Comedy	The Farce
		Act I	
Scenes	i, *ii*, iii, iv	v, vi, vii	viii
	M *ix*		x
		xi–xiv	
	xv–xviii		
		Act II	
	M i		ii
	iii, iv	v–vii	
	M viii, ix, x		xi
		xii, xiii, *xiv*	
	xv–xviii		
		Act III	
	M i		M ii
		iii–v	
	vi, vii	viii–xi	
	xii, xiii	*xiv*	xv
	M xvi		
Total number of scenes	25	21	6

(Italics indicate scenes in which persons of the drama and those of the comedy momentarily interact. M, "mutazione," indicates a new stage set.)

2. See especially II. xii–xiv.

The Sources

Librettos

Eraclea was performed at the Teatro San Bartolomeo, Naples, in 1700 and again, probably later in the same year, at Parma. The only known librettos are the ones printed for these two occasions:

N: L'ERACLEA / drama per musica / di Silvio Stampiglia / tra gli Arcadi / Palemone Licurio / dedicato / All'Ilustriss. & Eccellentiss. Signora / La Signora / D. MARIA / de Giron, y Sandoval / Duchessa di Medina-Celi, e / Viceregina di Napoli. / [Emblem] / In Napoli 1700 / Per Dom. Ant. Parrino, e Michele Luigi Mutio, / Con Licenza de' Superiori. / Si vende nella Stampa del Mutio, sita / allo Spedaletto
76 pages. Pp. 3–5, Stampiglia's dedicatory epistle; pp. 6–7, Argomento; pp. 8–9, Personaggi; p. 10, Mutazioni, Intermedii, and mention of Ferdinando Galli-Bibiena as designer of scenery. No mention of Scarlatti as composer.

P: L'ERACLEA / drama per musica / di Silvio Stampiglia / tra' gli Arcadi / Palemone Licurio. / Dedicato / all'Altezza Serenissima / di / FRANCESCO / Primo / Duca di Parma / [Emblem] / In Parma, M DCC. / Per Alberto Pazzoni, e Paolo Monti / Stampatori Ducali. / Con licenza de' Superiori.
100 pages. Pp. 5–6, dedicatory epistle signed Gioanni Tamagni; pp. 7–8, Argomento, [Protesta]; pp. 9–10, [Mutazioni], Intermezzi; p. 10, "La Musica, parte del Sig. Alessandro Scarlatti, parte del Sig. D. Bernardo Sabadini Maestro di Capella di S.A.S." and mention of Ferdinando Galli-Bibiena as designer of scenery; p. 11, Personaggi.

The intermedi at Naples, of which neither text, if any, nor music survives, were evidently simple ballets[3] quite unconnected with the action. Those at Parma, the texts of which appear in *P*, were much more elaborate: they brought onto the stage the two comic characters Livio and Alfeo in fantastic episodes involving sudden startling changes of scenery and including at one place a parody of a type of scene that had been a favorite in serious opera since the time of Cavalli, namely a conjuration of demonic spirits from the underworld. These extensive intermezzi at Parma were doubtless designed to compensate for the omission or curtailing of several of the comic scenes of the Naples version: thus, all of I.viii and II.x are omitted in *P*, and I.x lacks the two arias of *N*. *P* adds five arias not in *N* and substitutes new numbers for old in five other cases, transposes some scenes, omits passages of dialogue, and introduces numerous changes of detail.[4] The added and substituted numbers were probably composed by Sabadini; how much other music he wrote for the Parma *Eraclea* is not known because the score is apparently lost.

Scores

Scarlatti's *Eraclea* seems to have had only a brief career in the theater: no performances besides those at Naples and Parma are recorded, although the existence of seven more or less complete copies of the score would clearly imply that the separate numbers, or some of them, enjoyed a degree of favor in the eighteenth century. No music is preserved for the recitatives, save those in the comic scenes. The surviving music is found in the following eighteenth-century manuscript copies, all conforming to *N*.

3. I. Di Giochi di Picca, Bandiera, e Spada. II. Di Forze Diverse.
4. See Critical Notes to Nos. 2, 9, 28, 34, 37, 44, 49, 54, 56, 58, and 59, available from Department of Music, Harvard.

Br: Brussels, Bibliothèque royale de Belgique, Ms II. 3964 (*olim* Fétis 2521). 220 numbered folios; 19 × 26 cm.; same hand throughout. Title page:

Atto Primo: Arie / Dell'opera intitolata L'Eraclea / con Violini, Trombe, obuè, violette, Flauti, e Violoncelli. / Musica / del Sig.r Alessandro Scarlatti / Poesia / del Sig.r Silvio Stampiglia. 1700 [Upper right corner, in a different hand:] Eliz. Southwell

There is a transcript of this score in the Library of Congress (M 1500. S 28 E 6).

The Brussels manuscript was acquired by Fétis evidently between 1844 and 1865; beyond that, nothing is known of its provenience.[5] It is the most nearly complete of all the musical sources: of the three sinfonias, forty-six arias, ten duets, and four other ensembles of *N*, all but one are found in *Br* and, with one exception, in the same order as in the libretto. Moreover, *Br* contains the following numbers which are not in any of the other manuscripts: No. 12, the septet "Che maestà"; No. 22, Iliso's aria "Irene mi tradisce"; No. 26, the ensemble "Son nemici"; No. 27, the Sinfonia, in the same scene; No. 55, Eraclea's arioso "Contentatevi alemeno"; No. 60, Damiro's arioso "La tua sorte mi duole"; and No. 71, the closing ensemble "Alle gioie." All the manuscripts, including *Br*, lack the music for No. 66, the quartet in III.xiv; *Br* also lacks two of the added arias that are found in other sources: No. A2, Marcello's "Quanto è bella," which is in *Nc* and *Pn*, and No. A3, Flavia's "Questa nuova pena," which is found only in *Nc*. No. 70, the duet "Sei Lilla" is radically shorter in *Br* than in the other manuscripts.[6] In eleven arias and one duet in *Br* the orchestra is smaller than that called for in one or more of the other sources.[7]

These considerations support the presumption that *Br* is a reduced score; the orchestra has always the same musical material as in the other versions, but arranged for a smaller ensemble. Similarly, No. 70 is simply a shortened version of the duet. That *Br* includes only two of the four substitute arias, and those in an appendix, suggests that it derives from a relatively early version of the opera. That seven numbers in *Br* do not appear in any of the other manuscripts may be accounted for on various grounds. Eighteenth-century selections from operas— and this is the nature of all the sources of *Eraclea* except *Br*—as a rule comprise only arias and duets. Of the unica in *Br*, one is a sinfonia and three are ensembles requiring four to seven singers; the arioso No. 35, which comes at the beginning of a scene, is short and although beautiful musically is dramatically impertinent; it may well have been excised at a very early stage, whence its relegation to the appendix in *Br*. The arioso No. 60, which appears also at the beginning of a scene, is short, unfinished, old-fashioned in its use of an ostinato bass figure, dramatically awkward, and apparently corrupt in the musical text. No. 22 is also short and is the only aria in the entire opera for Iliso, a minor personage.

Nc: Naples, Biblioteca del Conservatorio S. Pietro di Majella, Sig. 266–34.5.12. 91 pages, with index on p. 92. Title page:

Arie del Dramma in 3 atti / Eraclea—Poesia di / Silvio Stampiglia—Musica di / Alessandro Scarlatti / Rappresentata in Napoli / al Teatro S. Bartolomeo / nel 1700

This is one of the numerous class of collections of arie scelte and the like intended for the use of individual virtuosi at semi-private gatherings. The volume contains thirty-three arias, three duets, and four "arie aggiunte" (not indexed) from *Eraclea*,

---

5. Information from Albert Vander Linden, Director of the Library of the Royal Conservatory of Music, Brussels.
6. See No. A5.
7. See Critical Notes to Nos. 5, 7, 11, 19, 20, 23, 25, 30, 31, 47, 53, and 65.

together with three duets and twenty-three cantatas from other sources. The handwriting is that of the copyist of eight other manuscripts, all dated between 1695 and 1701, containing arias and cantatas by Scarlatti and others.[8] Since this scribe invariably dated his manuscripts with the actual year of copying, it seems probable that *Nc* was made at Naples in 1700, when *Eraclea* was new. One may thus surmise that the music of the four arie aggiunte[9] is by Scarlatti himself and that these arias were used at the Naples performances, some of them possibly even from the beginning.

The order of contents in *Nc* has no apparent relation to the order of numbers in the libretto. No numbers from the comic scenes are included. The arias are written for soprano and figured bass, all but one of the six originally for contralto being transposed upward and written with the G-clef.[10] The bass, for the most part, is quite sparsely figured. One aria, No. 46, and one duet, No. 50, have a unisono violin part in addition to the bass. Instrumental introductions and interludes are frequently shortened or omitted; in some instances the bass line differs considerably from that in other sources.[11]

Lbm: London, British Museum RM 23.f.4. Nos. 29–50, ff. 50ᵛ–85ᵛ (pp. 98–168); foliation in ink, pagination in pencil; 19 × 26 cm. Described in the *Catalogue of the King's Music Library*, Part II, as follows: "Duets and arias . . . 55 vocal pieces, the first a Latin motet, the rest excerpts from Italian operas, written in the same hand throughout and by various composers. In score, with bass figured for harpsichord, and other instruments . . . ff 92. Paper, 18th century." The heading on f. 50ᵛ reads "Arie tirate dell' Eraclea Opera del Sig.r Alessandro Scarlatti, fatta nel anno 1700." Other composers named in this volume are Nicola Francesco Haim, Alessandro Stradella, Cesare Morelli, "S.r Abbate Stefano," Giovanni Bononcini (named as composer of an aria from the opera *Camilla trionfante*), Giovanni del Violine [*sic*], Luigi Rossi, and Carissimi.

Folios 50ᵛ–85ᵛ contain seventeen arias, five duets, and one sinfonia (No. 10), in random order. The handwriting is neat and close; the bass is sparsely figured. All items but the sinfonia and one duet occur also in *Pn.* It is possible that *Lbm* and *Pn* were copied from a common source: the number of exclusive common variants is fairly large. In five of the six numbers where the orchestration in *Lbm* differs from that in *Br, Lbm* and *Pn* correspond (Nos. 11, 23, 34, 53, 65); in the sixth, however (No. 64), the orchestra in *Lbm* differs from that of all the other manuscripts that contain this number in full score *(Br, Wn, Pn).*[12]

Wn: Vienna, Österreichische Nationalbibliothek SA 68.C.17, Nos. 1–16. 87 unnumbered pages in full score; same eighteenth-century hand throughout. Title page:
+ / Scelta d'Arie (16) / dell'opera Intitulata / ll'Eraclea / Poesia del sig.r Silvio / Stampiglia / musica del sig.r Alesandro / Scarlatti / nell' 1700 / [different hand:] Item Arie (22) dell'Opera Cesare in Alessandria [Naples, 1701] del Sign.r / Giuseppe Aldobrandini [i.e., Aldrovandini, ca. 1673–1708.]

---

8. Edwin Hanley of the University of California, Los Angeles, has most generously furnished me information about scribes and many valuable suggestions on other matters.
9. One of them appears only in this manuscript; see appendix A, Nos. A1–A4, and Critical Notes.
10. Nos. 8, 21, 33, 54, and 59.
11. See Nos. 5, 24, 37, and 47.
12. For details, see Critical Notes.

Wn contains, from *Eraclea*, the Sinfonia avanti l'Opera, twelve arias, and three duets in random order. The handwriting is ragged, and the score shows numerous errors. It is impossible from internal evidence to determine the relation of this to the other sources. *Wn* is the only manuscript other than *Br* that contains the Sinfonia avanti l'Opera. In the majority of its variants it corresponds to *Br*, but it has also some common variants with *Pn* and *Lbm*.

Pn: Paris, Bibliothèque Nationale (formerly Bibliothèque du Conservatoire) D 11836 (*olim* 4232). Index and 107 folios, 28.5 × 21 cm.; same eighteenth-century hand throughout. Title page:

Cantate / Del Sig.r D. [?] Alessandro Scarlatti / [upper right corner] Ce volume est composé des airs de l'opera Eraclea de Scarlatti, livret de Silvio Stampiglia, identifiés d'après le livret . . . publié à Naples en 1700. Reneé M. Masson, 31–1–57.

With the exception of *Br*, *Pn* is the most nearly complete of all the known copies of *Eraclea:* it contains forty-one arias and eight duets, including one substitute aria, No. A2, not in *Br*. Moreover, *Pn* gives in many cases what was probably the original orchestration of the accompaniments—in any case, fuller orchestration than is given in the corresponding numbers in *Br*. The writing is careless and full of errors.

The order of items in *Pn* contrasts with the haphazard arrangement of the preceding three manuscripts. Its contents come in blocks, eight in all, each containing from two to fourteen numbers in the same succession (disregarding omissions) as in *P;* the blocks themselves, however, do not follow one another according to any recognizable plan.[13]

One intriguing feature of *Pn* is its placement of the three arias, Nos. A1, A4, and A2, obviously substitutes for Nos. 36, 37, and 38, respectively. Whereas in *Br* and *Nc* all alternative arias are relegated to an appendix, in *Pn* these three occur consecutively and in precisely their proper location in the block containing Nos. 31–45; *Pn* nowhere contains the originals which these three were meant to replace, nor does either libretto contain the texts of these three substitute arias. One may conjecture that *Pn* was copied from a hypothetical score representing a stage in the opera's history after the substitutions had been definitely accepted and the originals dropped out; *Br* and *Nc*, on the other hand, would have been taken from a hypothetical earlier version, representing a stage at which the substitutions were still optional. *Lbm* and *Wn* contain neither the original nor the substitute arias. The situation with respect to all the substitute arias may be summarized thus:

A1 *(Br app., Nc app., Pn):* substitute for No. 36 *(Br, Nc)*
A2 *(Nc app., Pn):* substitute for No. 38 *(Br, Nc)*
A3 *(Nc app.):* substitute for No. 20 *(Br, Nc, Pn)*
A4 *(Br app., Nc app., Pn):* substitute for No. 37 *(Br, Nc)*

Dl: Dresden, Sächsische Landesbibliothek Mus. 1 / F / 39, 1. Folios 79–109. Title on f. 79: "Scene Buffe dell'Eraclea Del Sig.r Alessandro Scarlatti."

These folios contain five complete scenes: I.x, II.ii, II.xi, III.ii, and III.xv,

---

13. The blocks are highly uneven in length, and one of them begins on a verso page; therefore it is not a tenable hypothesis that *Pn* was once a fairly complete score rebound later with the gatherings in the wrong order. Moreover, it is impossible to determine from the present binding what any hypothetical original gatherings may have been. (Information from François Lesure, Bibliothèque Nationale.)

comprising in all eight recitatives, six arias, and five duets. The hand of the same scribe appears in copies of a serenata, arias, and a cantata by A. Scarlatti, a cantata by D. Scarlatti, and cantatas by Handel, all copied roughly within the period 1690 to 1710. *Dl* is the only source that preserves any of the secco recitatives from *Eraclea*, on which account it is uniquely valuable; furthermore, it frequently specifies tempo and instrumentation where the other manuscripts do not; and it alone provides closing ritornellos for four of the five comic duets (Nos. 18, 29, 43, 69). From inspection of common variants, it appears that *Dl* belongs to the same family of sources as *Pn* and *Lbm*.

The Dresden manuscript also contains "scene buffe" from other operas of Scarlatti: *Gli Inganni Felici* (1699), *Odoardo* (1700), *Tito Sempronio Gracco* (1702, 1720), *Il Pastor di Corinto* (1701), *Dafni e Galatea* (1700); and from two operas of G. Aldrovandini: *Semiramide* (1701) and *Cesare in Alessandria* (1701). All the foregoing except *Semiramide* were first presented at Naples.

Cm: Cambridge, Pepys Library, Magdalene College, PL 1807. 197 numbered folios; 8.5 × 23 cm. On f. 1:

Eraclea. / Opera / In Napoli. / A⁰ 1700.

On front endpaper is Pepys's small portrait-bookplate; on f. 196ᵛ is Pepys's anchor-bookplate.[14]

Cm contains forty-six arias and duets for voice(s) and unfigured bass, including one aria not found in any other source and a shorter version of the first part of the duet No. 50. Only enough of the bass is put in to give cues to the singer. Most of its frequent errors, omissions, and octave displacements have not been listed in the Critical Notes; likewise omitted are details of the irregular barring of fast arias in C 3/8 or C 3/4, which often differ without apparent reason from the barring in the other sources.

Editorial Procedure

The aim of this edition is to present an accurate version of the score as the composer delivered it, with only those notational changes necessary to make it more easily readable by modern players and singers. All places where the edition differs materially from one or more of the sources are listed in the Critical Notes. Obvious trivial errors have been corrected without notice. Bracketed notes in the continuo of Nos. 7, 34, and 41 are lacking in some sources.

Division by acts and scenes is shown in the table of contents. Musical items in the score are numbered consecutively throughout the opera. Headings in italics are editorial designations, for example, aria, duetto; more specific designations, such as aria buffa, are given only where such exist in one or more of the sources.

The text has been lightly edited, especially with respect to accents, capitalization, and punctuation, to conform somewhat more closely to modern Italian usage. Archaic words have been retained; spelling in general has been modernized. Contractions not in present use have been eliminated: thus, brev'ora becomes breve ora, gl'amici becomes gli amici. In cases where it seemed that the distribution of syllables might cause difficulty, elisions have been marked.

Measures are numbered beginning with the first complete measure. Irregular barrings, for example, mixtures of 3/8 and 6/8, have been made regular, departures from the original being signalized in the Critical Notes. Dots across

14. See H. B. Wheatley, *Diary of Samuel Pepys*, supplementary volume *Pepysiana* (London, 1897), p. 63.

barlines, and occasionally dots across strong beats, have been rendered by ties. Triplets, sometimes in the original [♩.=♪♪♪], have been modernized to [♩=♪♪♪], and similarly for smaller values. No attempt has been made to reproduce the copyists' beaming of notes in the instrumental parts.

The superfluous C has been dropped from meter signatures such as C 3/4, C 3/8. Original key signatures are retained and added accidentals indicated according to modern usage. In the voice parts soprano and alto C-clefs become treble clef, tenor C-clef, a tenor G-clef; C-clefs in the viola and solo violoncello parts and, as a rule, the occasional tenor C-clef in the basso continuo, remain.

Indications for tempo and dynamics are reproduced only if they appear in at least one manuscript. Editorially added slurs or ties are marked thus: ⌣ . The sign ⌣‖ in the bass of recitatives indicates tied notes that are separated in the source by reason of a divided measure.

Specification of instruments is supplied by the editor; in any doubtful cases, names that appear in the sources are listed in the Critical Notes. As a rule, the string parts and continuo have no special designation in the sources; a single undesignated instrumental line with a G-clef has been assumed to be for violins unisoni.

Three arias (Nos. 9, 21, 33) and one duet (No. 29) having a meter signature of C with consistent triple subdivision of the beat have been transcribed in 12/8, with the following equivalences:[15]

Manuscripts	Edition

Figures for the continuo, whatever their location in the manuscripts, have been placed in this edition below the staff. For the most part these figures are taken from *Br*; figures in parentheses occur only in *Pn* (for exceptions, see Critical Notes); italicized figures are editorial. I have not usually distinguished between 43 and 4̶3 , since these two signs are often indistinguishable in the copies and frequently vary from one manuscript to another.

Almost always at the end of a vocal number the copyists write "Da capo" with a brief cue. I have omitted the cues and, where needful, expressed the in-

---

15. See Michael Collins, "The Performance of Triplets in the 17th and 18th Centuries," *Journal of the American Musicological Society* 19 (1966):281–328; Robert Donington, *The Interpretation of Early Music*, 2d ed. (London, 1965), pp. 398–403.

tention by a Dal segno. "Fine" in this edition is indicated simply by a fermata over the last note or rest of the A section in all the parts. In a few instances a Da capo will be written out in one or more of the sources, occasionally in modified or shortened form. Rarely, no Da capo is called for.[16]

Notes on Performance Practice

Ornaments

Italian opera composers of the early eighteenth century counted on singers having been trained to add embellishments to the written notes. Such embellishments were either introduced spontaneously at the moment of performance or else designed and executed so as to give an impression of spontaneity. No two singers, probably, would embellish a melody in quite the same way, nor would any singer repeat exactly the same embellishments at every performance. The essential qualities of spontaneity and variety cannot be achieved by freezing a certain set of embellishments in notation; singers now as in earlier times must learn to supply them with freedom and good taste within certain general rules. Just how many ornaments should be added to the arias in *Eraclea* is uncertain; my opinion is that not very many are needed. Most of the frequently cited examples of elaborate vocal ornamentation in the eighteenth century come from a period later than that of Scarlatti.[17]

The most common ornament is the appoggiatura, usually followed by some form of trill, at important dominant-tonic cadences. In many cases, Scarlatti has written the appoggiatura into the melodic line; where he has not, it may be added. (See Example 1.) A special case of the cadential appoggiatura occurs in recitative

Example 1

No. 11, mm. 34-36

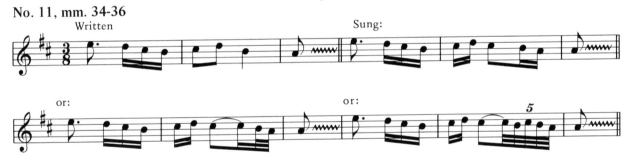

cadences where the voice descends by a third to the final. (See Example 2.) At final and semifinal dominant-tonic cadences in recitative, the chords over the penultimate bass note (figured 43 or 4₃) may be taken either with the singer—thereby producing momentary dissonances if the vocal cadence is like that of Example 2—or after he has finished, depending on the tempo of the dialogue.[18]

16. Nos. 6, 38, and 55 have written-out Da capos in some of the sources. Nos. 12, 45, 54, and 69 have no Da capo.
17. For a comprehensive survey of this and other features of performance practice in Renaissance and Baroque music, with copious citations from contemporary theorists and a valuable annotated bibliography of sources and modern studies, see Donington, *Intrepretation of Early Music.*
18. For an illuminating though not conclusive discussion of this matter with reference to sources and modern studies, see S. H. Hansell, "The Cadence in Eighteenth-Century Recitative," *Musical Quarterly* 54 (1968):228–248.

Example 2

No. 52, m. 34

Other ornaments, such as trills, turns, passing tones, short appoggiaturas, and mordents, may be introduced into arias where appropriate. The following general principles apply: the melody must not be obscured; ornaments must be consistent with the harmony and the general mood of the piece, avoiding excess; they are more appropriate in slow than in fast movements; when used they should progress from few to more in the course of a number. Thus, a Da capo aria could take additional ornamentation at the repetition of its first part: for example, in No. 25, mm. 16–30, possibly as shown in Example 3. The only ornaments specifically indicated in any manuscript of *Eraclea* are those in mm. 21–22 of No. 7 and the trills in Nos. 34, 48, 55, and 57.

Instruments

Strings and harpsichord will be the foundation of the orchestra; violins may be doubled by oboes and the bass line by one or two bassoons in fast movements of sinfonias and in most loud arias; a violone or bassoon may be added to the bass line in some other arias; recitatives and other numbers with only continuo accompaniment will ordinarily use harpsichord and solo violoncello or gamba. Specific indications for instruments are scarce and often vary from one manuscript to another; in performance, a single-line violin part may be taken by all the violins unisoni, or by firsts or seconds only, or even by a solo violin. Instrumentation may change in the course of a number, for example, being made fuller at ritornellos. Obbligato flutes (that is, recorders) are required in the accompaniments of Nos. 53 and 56, obbligato trumpet(s) in those of Nos. 11 (also oboes), 26, and 48. Violas are divided in No. 20, violoncellos in Nos. 31 and 48.

Which passages should be performed senza cembalo is uncertain. No such direction appears anywhere in the manuscripts of *Eraclea*. However, it should be remembered that neither the absence of a particular staff for the basso continuo, nor the absence of figures, nor notation in the tenor clef, nor any combination of these factors necessarily implies that the cembalo should be silent. A part written in the tenor clef is sometimes figured where the continuo rests, as in No. 48. The bass line of No. 30, which in *Nc* is written almost entirely unfigured and in the tenor clef, is there expressly marked "Violoncello e cembalo." Sometimes the sources disagree as to the texture of the accompaniment.[19] Some passages with no notated continuo sound thin and ineffective without the cembalo (for example, the introduction of No. 31). The two continuo parts in No. 25 suggest the probably common presence in Scarlatti's orchestra of a second cembalo, useful particularly in antiphonal passages or to go with the concertizing instruments in

---

19. See Critical Notes to Nos. 34, 41, and elsewhere.

Example 3

No. 25, mm. 16-30

accompaniments, as in No. 47. Probably the least ambiguous case for an entire aria senza cembalo is No. 64, with its pure trio texture of violin, voice, and violoncello, although even here some sources seem to suggest a regular accompaniment with continuo, and one adds a full orchestral ritornello.

Dynamics and tempo

Specific indications are sparse and variable. In general, a dynamic marking in one orchestral part applies to all. In arias, as a rule the orchestra plays forte in introductions, interludes, and ritornellos, and piano when accompanying the voice. Crescendo and diminuendo, never indicated in the manuscripts, may be used where appropriate, as often in slow arias; many fast arias, on the other hand, evidently call for terrace dynamics. An immediate repetition of a short phrase is generally understood to be piano (echo effect); occasionally the *p* will be found as a reminder, either in the voice part or, less often, in the accompaniment.

Eighteenth-century tempo indications are to be taken in a general sense: allegro means bright, cheerful, not necessarily very fast (presto is used for that); similarly, adagio does not always mean so slow a tempo as is implied by the word in modern usage. Meter signatures may convey some indication of tempo: ₵, C with triplet subdivision, and 3/8 are usually fast; 12/8 in a minor key is slow, but 12/8 in major, C, and 3/4 do not carry precise or consistent implications for tempo. The decision in each case, of course, must be based ultimately on the character of the music itself.

Tempo in the comic recitatives must be lively and flexible, depending on the rhythm of the sentences and the natural pace of the dialogue rather than on precise note values. The essential is that these numbers be recited in music, not sung like arias.

Rhythm

Certain rhythmic conventions of the early eighteenth century apply to the music of *Eraclea*. The first is the practice called double-dotting or overdotting, that is, prolonging a dotted note at the expense of the shorter note following. Overdotting is not to be applied indiscriminately. It is most appropriate in vigorous allegro passages where a dotted rhythmic figure dominates the movement, as in Nos. 11, 44, 48, and 67. (See Example 4a.) A rest replacing the first note in such a figure is likewise overdotted. (See Example 4b.) In quieter passages with this rhythm the dots may be prolonged, though less emphatically, as in Nos. 5, 30, and 64. Sometimes a dot must be prolonged in order to avoid unnatural inconsistencies of rhythm between two simultaneous lines (No. 64, mm. 9 and 35, second beat in the strings; m. 24, third beat in the voice; the sixteenth rest in the bass at m. 20 should not be dotted). Similarly, notes may sometimes be dotted, or dots removed, to preserve rhythmic consistency among the several voices (No. 5, mm. 4–6, 16–17).

Example 4

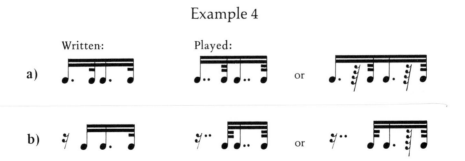

14

The convention of *notes inégales*—that is, of alternately lengthening and shortening in performance notes which are written in even lengths—applies less often to Italian than to French music in this period. There are only a few places in *Eraclea* where it clearly seems to be in order: for example, the beamed sixteenth-note groups in the voice at mm. 12–13 and 22–26 of No. 44, and some or perhaps all of the two- and four-note groups of sixteenths in both voice and orchestra of No. 65. Variants among the sources sometimes furnish a clue pointing in this direction: the variants among the manuscripts of No. 70, for example, as well as the rhythm of the continuo, suggest that all the sixteenth-note groups were meant to be sung unequally. Other places for applying inequality may doubtless be found if one is inclined to favor this particular device, but on the whole, a policy of restraint in this matter is advisable with Scarlatti's music.[20] Certainly no liberties should be taken with No. 48 except to overdot the initial rhythmic figure wherever it occurs; the conflict between this and the rhythm of the even sixteenths and triplets is one of Scarlatti's means of depicting the "battaglia" of the text.

20. One argument for a more liberal application of *notes inégales* might be derived from a singular discrepancy among the sources of No. 30. Six of the seven manuscripts that contain this aria notate the dotted figure in the accompaniment exactly as we have transcribed it in this edition; the seventh, *Br*, gives it in even sixteenth-notes throughout.

ERACLEA

Cast of Characters

Eraclea	soprano
Flavia ⎫ Eraclea's daughters	soprano
Irene ⎭	alto
Decio, Capuan noble, disguised as a woman under the name Aldimira	soprano
Marcello, Roman consul	soprano
Damiro, Syracusan noble	soprano
Iliso, Syracusan noble	tenor
Livio, Decio's page, disguised as a woman under the name Lilla	soprano
Alfeo, tutor of Flavia and Irene	bass

Scene: Syracuse; Eraclea's palace and environs
Time: 212 B.C.

1. Sinfonia avanti L'Opera

Tutti all' Unisoni

19

ATTO PRIMO

ATTO PRIMO

2. Aria a 2 Voci

mi par che sia quest'al - ma non ben tor -

ques - to seno in-gom - bra qualche om - bra di ti -mor,

na-ta in cal - ma

e ques -to seno ingom - bra qualche om-bra di ti - mor⸻, di timor.

Da capo

3. Aria

Violino I

Violino II

Eraclea

Sto pur dub - bio-sa, che far non so; dub - bio - sa sto, che far non

Continuo

Decio

Eraclea

so. Ris-pon - di, alma a-do - ra-ta. Tut - ta agi - ta - ta io mi con -

[recitative]

[in tempo]

26

fon - do, e non ri - spon - do ne sì, ne no;

e non ri - spon - do ne sì, ne no. Ri - spon - di, ri - spon - di.

[Decio]

Da capo

4. Aria con Violini all' Unisoni

Sa - prò, sa - prò pu-pil-le ca - re, ca-re pu-pil-le ca-re, ca-re sa-pròserbare a - mo-re, si-

len - zio e ser-vi - tù; pu-pil-le ca-re, ca-re, ca - re, ca - re sa-prò ser-

bare a - mo - re, a - mo - re si - len - zio   si - len-zio e ser - vi - tù

ca - re sa-prò ser - bare a - mo - re, a mo - re si - len - zio,   si-len-zio e ser-vi - tù.

Co-me sa-prà il mio co - re   ser-vir,   ta - ce - re   e a - ma - re lo scor-ge-

rai _____, lo scor - ge - rai ben tu;   co-me sa-pra ser-

vir, co-me sa-prà ta-cer e co-me saprà a-ma - re lo scor-ge-rai,   lo scor - ge - rai   ben tu.   Sa-

Dal segno

5. Aria

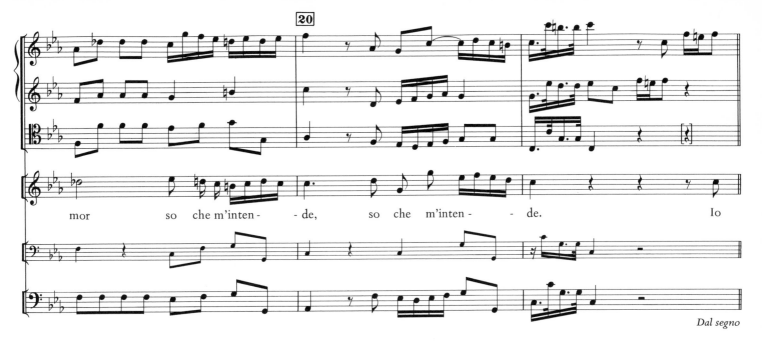

mor - so che m'inten - - de, so che m'inten - - de. Io

Dal segno

6. Aria Buffa

Alfeo

guardando Lilla

Bi - so - gna con giu -di - zi - o fug - gir sem-pre il periglio. (Che boc - ca, o Dio, che

Continuo

[recitative]

ci - glio! Al - feo, Al - feo, sta sa -ldo.) Amor ha un bratto vi - zi - o, ha un brutto

[in tempo]

vi - zi - o d'avvele - nar lo stra - le. (In - som - ma l'uomo è fra - le, l'uomo è fra - le, mi

[recitative]

sento venir caldo, mi sento venir cal - do, mi se-nto venir caldo.) Bi -

[in tempo]

31

so-gna con giu-di-zi-o fug-gir sem-pre il pe-ri-glio. (Che boc- ca, o Dio, che

[recitative]

ci -glio! Al - feo, Al - feo, sta sa -ldo.) Con giu-di-zi -o... (Che boc - ca!) fug -

[in tempo]

gir sem-pre il pe - ri - glio. (Che ciglio! Alfeo, Al - feo, Alfeo, sta saldo, sta saldo.)

7. *Aria*

Allegro

Violino I

Violino II

Viola

Flavia — Non vo - glio, non vo - glio, non

Continuo

voglio, non vo-glio ge-lo-si - a ma so-lo, so-lo vo - glio, ma so-lo voglio a - mor;

non vo - glio ge-lo - sia ma so-lo vo-glio, vo-glio so - lo, ma so-lo voglio a -

mor, ma so-lo vo-glio, vo-glio so - lo, ma so-lo vo-glio amor, voglio a - mor.

e all' al -ma pia - ce - ri - a che m'ucci - des - se, che m'ucci - des - se ognor, e all'

al - ma pia - ce - ria che m'ucci -des -se____, che m'ucci -desse o - gnor.

Da capo

8. *Aria*

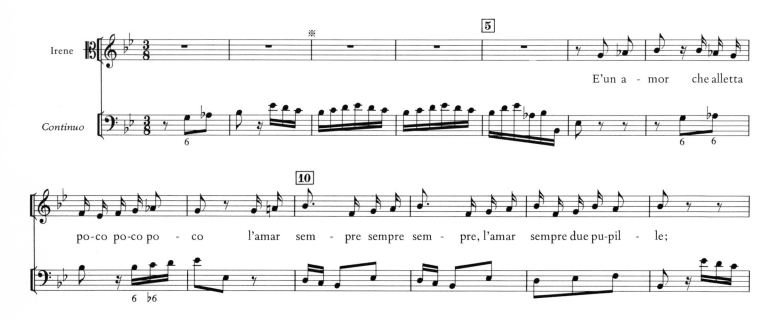

E' un a - mor che alletta

po-co po-co po - co l'amar sem - pre sempre sem - pre, l'amar sempre due pu-pil - le;

9. Aria

E' pur strano veder con la
gon - na un ra - gazzo che faccia da don - na stra - sci - na - re___ tre
pa - lme, tre palmi di co - da; è strano ve - der con la
gon - na un ra - gaz - zo che fac - cia da don - na stra - sci - na - re, stra - sci -
na - re tre palmi di co - da, stra - sci - na - re tre palmi di co - da.
Mi con - vie - ne sa - permi in - chi - na - re, sa - per - mi inchi - na - re,

10. Sinfonia con Trombe e Violini

per lo Sbarco di Marcello

Segue l'Aria con Istromti

11. Aria

Spie-gan sem - - - - - pre le na-vi la-ti-ne bel-le

che le gui - da col bion - do suo cri - ne_____ dove il

Fa - - - - - - - - - -to gran pre - de, gran pre - de le a - du -

na,   dove il Fa - - - - - - - - - - -

- to gran pre-de, gran pre-de le a-du - na.

Spie-gan

Dal segno

12. Aria a 7

43

13. Recitativo

Segue l'Aria

44

15. *Recitativo*

(O che impu-lsi, o che gua-i.) E dove trove-rai u-na sposet-ta o Di - o, a-mo-ro-sa co-

sì co-me so-no i - o? Per te di pian-to a - sper - go l'uno e l'a-ltro mio ci - glio. (O Dio, quel

er - go.) Deh pen-sa a ca-si tuo - i: se contrar - re non vuoi que-sti I-me-ne - i si

per-de-rà la raz-za de-gli Al-fe - i. (Sen - so, sen-so ri - bal - do, più non pos-so star sal-do.)

E mi vor-rai ve - de-re me-sta co-sì? (Non pos - so più te-ne - re.)

Segue

16. *Aria*

17. *Recitativo*

Mia gio - ia, mio de - si - re. Non più, non più, che tu mi fai mo - ri - re.

In te sol mi ri - cre - o. (Non stare ab - ban - do - na - to a - ni - mo, a - ni - mo Al - fe - o.)

18. *Duetto*

Mi sento ardito, ar - di - to sen - to, sen - to sento mi sen - to ar - dito, ar -

S'è rim - bam - bi - to, s'è messo in mo -

di - to, tut - to mi scuo - to, tut - to tut - to tut - to mi scuo - to.

to. Non v'a - gi - ta - te, non v'a - gi -

Mio ben, mio ben che fa - te?

Ritornello

19. *Aria*

Io non di-co che tu non sei bel-la, che tu non sei bel-la,

di - co sol, di - co sol che è de - sti - - no, è de - sti - no l'a -

mo - re, l'a - mo - - - re; non di - co non sei bel - la, di - co sol che è de -

sti - - - no, è de - sti - no l'a - mo - re, l'a - mo - - - re.

Non è il ge - nio che for - za di stel - la

ed a quel-la sog - gia - ce, sog - gia-ce o - gni co - - re, è

for - za di stel-la, ed a quel-la sog - gia-ce o - gni co - - re_____. Io non

Dal segno

20. *Aria*

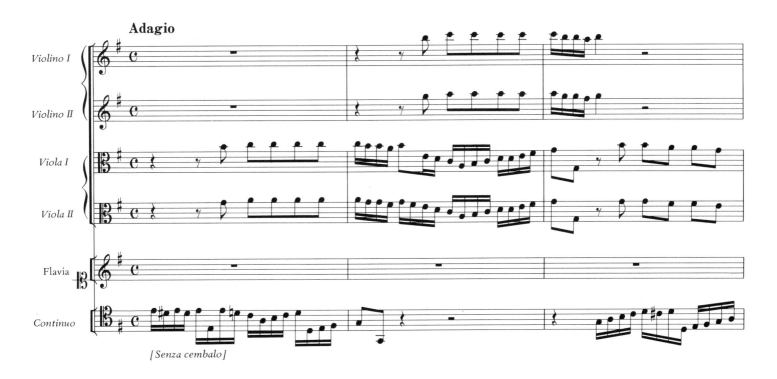

A que-sto nuo-vo af-fan — no tut — ta s'abbando- nò _____ ,

[Con cembalo]

tut - ta s'abbandonò _____ l'a - - - -ni-ma mi - a, l'a - - -

21. *Aria*

Mi pia-ci sì, ma tu se fos-si men ge-lo-so mi pia-ce-re-sti più, mi

pia-ci sì, ma tu se fos-si men ge-lo-so mi pia-ce-re-sti più, ma tu se

fos-si men ge-lo-so mi pia-ce-re-sti più. Se volgo ad uno i guar-di, se

muo-vo i lab-bri a ri-so, tor-bi-do tu mi guar-di, tut-to ti can-gi in vi-so, e di-ci che amo-ro-il

guardo e il ri-so,il guar-do e il ri-so fu,— e di-ci che amo-ro-so il guar-do e il ri-so fu.

Da capo

56

22. Aria

Iliso: I - re - ne mi tra - di - sce e no'l do - vria mai far, I - re - ne mi tra - di - sce, mi tra-di - sce e no'l do - vria____, e no'l do - vria____ mai far, e no'l do - vria mai far. Per lei se tutta a - mo-re quest'a - - ni - ma lan - gui - sce, e come ha tan - to co - re, co - - me mi può ingan-nar, co - - me mi può ingan-nar, mi può in-gan-nar?

Da capo

23. Aria

Decio: Ri - cor-dati che io t'a - mo e ser-vo e tac - cio____, che io t'amo e ser - vo e servo e tac - cio____, ri -

cordati che io t'a - mo e servo e tac - cio_____, ricordati che io t'a - mo e servo e tac - cio.

E se hai pietà di me___ non mi mancar di fè ___, che io vi - ve - re non bra - mo ad altra in brac -

cio___, che io vi - ve - re non bra - mo ad altra in brac - cio ___, ad al - - - tra, ad altra in brac - cio ___. Ri-

Dal segno

24. *Aria*

25. Aria

mor   mi la - - - - - - gno,   mi lagno anch'i -

o,   mi la - - - - - - - gno,   mi lagno anch'i -

Ar - don d'a-mor le stel - le, le pian - te, i

sas - si, il fio - re, lan - gui - sco - no d'a - mo - re le

me - ste tor - to - rel - le, e in - na - mo - ra - to ba -

ATTO SECONDO

26. Ensemble

te - me vero a - mor non sa che si - a,

Eraclea

Eraclea, Marcello, Decio

Son ne - mici e vanno in - sie - me, e l'a - more e ge - lo - si - a, son ne - mici e vanno in -

Flavia, Irene, Damiro, Iliso

Son ne - mici e vanno in -

-sie - me, e l'a - more e ge - lo - si - a, vanno in - sie - me, e l'a - more e ge - lo - si - a,

-sie - me, e l'a - more e ge - lo - si - a, vanno in - sie - me, e l'a - more e ge - lo - si - a,

27. Sinfonia

28. Recitativo

Al-feo giun-ge-sti tar-di. Già finito è il tri-pu-di-o? Sì, ma do-ve fi-no-ra? Son sta-to in stu-di-o: dim-mi Lil-la, chi c'e-ra? C'e-ra l'uo-mo, la don-na, la co-sa fo-ra-stie-ra. Sempre, sempre coi tuoi stram-bot-ti. Io con gli uo-mi-ni dot-ti di-scor-rer so-glio in pun-ta di for-chet-ta. A — Lil-let-ta, Lil-let-ta. Quan-to sei ca-ro, sa-po-ri-to, e gai-o. Mi vie-ne per la vi-ta il for-mi-cai-o. Per-chè ti stor-ci tan-to? Lil-la non star-mi ac-can-to. Per qual ra-gion? Par-lan-do con mo-de-sti-a, se vado in be-sti-a, non a-vrai ri-pa-ro. Che di-ven-ti ta-lor lu-po man-na-ro?

Segue

29. Aria Buffa a 2

30. *Aria*

La mia ti - ran - na,

la mia ti - ran - na è ge - lo - si - a, è ge - lo - si - a, ge - lo - si -

stil-la in se - no, que-sta m'af-flig - ge, que-sta m'af-fan - na, que-sta tra -

fig - ge l'a - ni-ma, l'a - ni-ma mi - a, que-sta m'af-flig - ge, que-sta m'af -

fan - na, que-sta tra-fig - ge l'a - ni-ma, l'a - ni-ma mi - a. La mia ti -

Dal segno

79

Que - sti co - ri se A - mo - re can -

32. Aria

33. Aria

Più non ti vo-glio no, più non mi pia - ci, più non ti vo-glio no, più non mi pia - ci, non ti vo - glio, non mi pia - ci, non ti vo-glio no no no___, più non mi pia - ci, no no,___ più non mi pia - ci.

Se un tempo eri il mio bel - lo, ed or non sei più quel - lo, dim - mi, che far si può?

Sof-fri-lo, sof-fri-lo_____ e ta - ci, sof-fri - lo, sof-fri - lo_____ e ta - ci.

Da capo

34. *Aria*

Violino solo

Violoncello *solo*

Flavia

Chi la - scia la sua bel - la,

Continuo

chi la - scia la sua bel - la e un' al - tra, un' al - tra a - mar ne vuo -

le, per-den-do e que-sta e quel - la, per-den-do e que-sta e quel - la re - sta,

resta deluso un dì; chi las-cia la sua bel-la e un al-tra a-mar ne vuo-le, per-dendo e que-sta e quel - la re - - - - - - - - sta, re-sta de-lu - so, de-lu - so un dì.

A un in-co-stan-te a-man-te so

che più vol-te suo - le suc - ce-de - re co-sì, a un in-co-stan-te a- man-te so

che più vol-te suo - le suc - ce-de - re co-sì, co - sì, co - sì, suc - ce-de - ra co-sì.

Da capo

35. *Arioso*

Adagio

Violino I
Violino II
Eraclea
Con-tenta-te-vi al-me - no miei pensieri amoro-si, che io pren-da nel dor-mir, che io
Continuo

pren-da nel dor-mir dol - ci, dol - ci ri-po-si.

Da capo

rà   ti spia - ce - rà,   ti spia - ce - rà.

Non ti ve - drai solo in a -

mo-re no   non ti ve-drai solo in a - mo-re ma tro-ve - rai___ ri - va - li -

-tà, ma trove - rai ri -va - li - tà.   Sa-per tu

Dal segno

38. *Aria*

39. Aria Buffa

40. *Recitativo*

Livio: Lil - la   a te s'av - vi - ci - na. Ec - co la mia ru - i - na; non me ne so dar pa - ce.

Livio: Dim - mi   for - se ti spi - ace,   che agli amo - ro - si sguar - di   ri - so - lu - to ti

sei   di ar - der sì tar - di?   Son sta - to sal - do tan - ti lu - stri,   e poi

vi - sta la fac - cia tua bru - net - ta e bel - la   non sce - si no, pre - ci - pi - tai di sel - la.   Or che tu sei ca - du - to

fa - rai mai più con Fla - via e con I - re - ne   il Sa - tra - po di A - te - ne?   E' sem - pre

ben dar buon con - si - glio agli al - tri.   Fan mol - ti vec - chi scal - tri   i cor - ret - to - ri del - la gio - ven -

tù, son tut-ti, tut-ti vi-zio, e fin-go-no vir-tù. Strano è an-cora il ve-

de-re certe donne at-tem-pa-te far da va-ghe, da bel-le, da morte in-na-mo-ra-te, e da don-

zel-le, e se poi fa l'a-mor qual-che ra-gaz-za le dan no-me di paz-za,

tut-te si scan-da-liz-za-no, e tan-te ciar-le in-fil-za-no, che è co-sa da stor-di-re;

e lo-ro? E lo-ro poi... nol vo-glio di-re. Questo è un caso che spes-so suc-ce-de-rà, suc-

ce-de ed è suc-ces-so; io pe-rò che ho cervello m'at-tac-co al bono, al gio-va-netto e al bel-lo.

Segue Aria con V.V.

41. Aria Buffa

42. *Recitativo*

Alfeo: Lil-la mia, Lil-la ta-ci, tutta a genio mi vai, tut-ta, tut-ta mi pia-ci, tu per i den-ti miei ca-ra mia gio-ia sei giu-sto un bi-scot-ti-no di Sa-vo-ia. Tu per far-mi sa-tol-la un gran pa-stic-cio

Alfes: sei di pa-sta frol-la.

Livio: Quel vol-to mo-ret-ti-no, o po-ten-za del mon-do è pur di-vi-no, mi pare un ciel di chia-ro oscuro a-dor-no tal qua-le sta sullo spuntar del giorno. Al manto, al-la fi-gu-ra, al-la gra-ve strut-tu-ra, a quel ventre di Bac-co mi res-sembri l'i-dea dell'Almanacco.

Alfeo: Io di tut-to m'in-tendo, posso de contin-gentibus fu-tu-ris dar certis-sime nove, e so quando è bon tempo e quando piove.

Segue a 2

100

te, vi -ta per te.　　(E' trop -po

te, co -re per te.　　(E' mas-si-mo　　il

Adagio

lo spas - so.) Mio dol - ce sci - rop - po, già pas - so, mer-cè

gu - sto.) Mio dol - ce sci - rop - po, già mo - ro, soc-cor - so, mo-ro

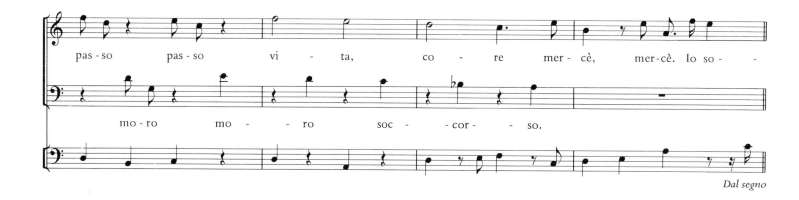

pas - so pas - so vi - ta, co - re mer - cè, mer-cè. Io so -

mo - ro mo - ro soc - cor - so.

Dal segno

Ritornello

Violino I

Violino II

Viola

Continuo

102

44. Duetto

che I - li - so non a - mi

e fol - le de - li - ro e gran va - ni - tà, e gran va - ni - tà

mi - ro
è fol - le de - li - ro
e gran va - ni - tà, e gran va - ni - tà

, è gran va - ni - tà

, è gran va - ni - tà

, è gran va - ni - tà.
Ma

è gran va - ni - tà.
Ma
Da - mi - ro mi pia - ce,

Dal segno

45. *Duetto*

Violino I, II

Damiro

Quando è d'a-mor l'er - ro - re
Quando è d'a-mor l'er

Iliso

Continuo

46. Aria

Non vuò, non vuò pietà da lei, vo - glio, vo - glio, vo - glio pietà da te, vo - glio

vo - glio, vo - glio pietà da te____, non vuò pie-tà da lei,____ da te vo -glio pie - tà, pie - tà____

____, vo - glio pietà da te, pie-tà_____, vo - grio pietà da te. Se la mia vi - ta

sei, sei vi - ta mi - a____ non mi ne-gar mer - cè____, non mi ne-gar mer - cè____, se la mia vi - ta

sei, sei vi - ta mi - a, non mi ne-gar mer - cè____, non mi ne-gar mer - cè____, non mi negar mer - cè_____. Non

Dal segno

Dal segno

48. Aria

111

glo - ria e l'a - mo - re; nel mio pet - to con fie - ra bat -

ta - - - - glia, fan - no guer - - -

ma non so di chi fia la vit-to-ria, so che mai nè là-

-mor nè la glo-ri-a non dan tre-gua, non dan tre-gua al mio

po-ve-ro co-re, al mio po-ve-ro co-

re. Nel mio

Dal segno

114

ATTO TERZO

ATTO TERZO

49. *Aria*

Violino I, II

Eraclea

In - gan - na - to - re, a - nima in - fi - da, in - gan - na - to - re, a - ni - ma in -

Continuo

fi - da, a - - - - - ni - ma,

a - nima in - fi - da, a - - ni - ma in - fi - da.

Se ol - trag - gi A - mo - re A - mor t'uc - ci - da, A - mor t'uc - ci - da.

A - mor, A - mor t'uc - ci - da, A - mor, A - mor t'uc - ci - da.

Da capo

117

50. Duetto

51. Aria Buffa

Con mo - der - na sim - me - tri - a si ve - sti, si ve -
sti l'an - ti - chi - tà, con mo - der - na sim - me - tri - a si ve - sti, si ve - sti l'an - ti - chi - tà.

Da capo

52. *Recitativo*

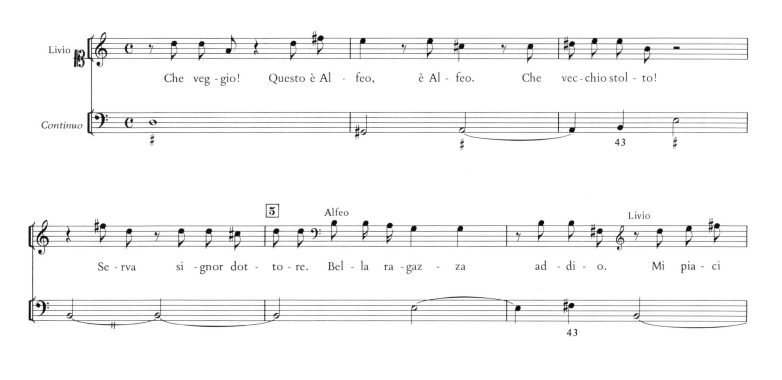

Livio

Che veg - gio! Questo è Al - feo, è Al - feo. Che vec - chio stol - to!

Continuo

43

Alfeo

Livio

Se - rva si - gnor dot - to - re. Bel - la ra - gaz - za ad - di - o. Mi pia - ci

43

molto, col par-ruc-co-ne e con il giu-sta-co-re. Mi son ve-stito al-l'u-so,

e sot-to e so-pra, sol per la tu-a bel-lez-za. Questa è trop-pa fi-nez-za, el-la si co-pra.

Or vor-rei ca-ro Al-feo, sa-per se tu sai far da ci-cis-be-o.

Non vi son co-se nuo-ve per un che tan-to sa. Dun-que, dun-que al-le pro-ve. Os-

ser-va, os-ser-va che ma-nie-ra a-gile e de-stra. Fi-gu-ra-ti ve-

Fanno molti atti muti
amoreggiando tra loro.

der-mi al-la fi-ne-stra. Bra-vo, bra-vo as-sa-i. Che ti pa-re?

Tut-to, tut-to san fa-re le per-so-ne dot-te. Or fi-gu-ra-ti tu che sia di not-te.

Livio

Be-ne ti par che va-da? Sì. Fin-gi a-des-so d'in-con-trar-mi in stra-da.

Alfeo *Tornano ad amoreggiare.* Livio

Come sopra.

Dim-me-la giu-sta, in far da va-go io sce-glio gli at-ti più pro-prii? Non si

Alfeo Livia

può far me-glio. Mi co-man-da la sor-te che io sia lo spo-so tu-o. Tu mio con-sor-te?

Alfeo Livio

Ci hai re-pu-gnan-za al-cu-na? An-zi è mia gran for-tu-na, per-chè se-ra, e mat-ti-na

Alfeo Livio

sot-to là tua dot-tri-na di-sci-pli-na-ta Lil-la, un gior-no di-ver-rà sa-via Si-bil-la.

Sa - rai dot - ta, e sa - ga - ce in po - chi dì per - chè tu sei ca - pa - ce. Ma_

_ gio - ia mi - a quan - do fa - rem tra no - i le noz - ze che de - si - o? Quan - do tu vuo - i. A -

- des - so. Flem - ma, flem - ma, dam - mi un tan - tin di tem - po. Sbri - ga - ti, mio te -

- so - ro più pre - sto che tu puoi per - chè, per - chè mi mo - ro. Dun - que per me tu

sen - ti.... Di - lu - vii di tor - men - ti, non ho un'o - ra di be - ne, e de - gli af - fan - ni

Presto

miei, chi va, chi vie - ne, chi va _____, chi va, chi vie - ne.

Segue a 2 con Varii Stromenti

124

53. Duetto

pur com-pas-sio - ne,   son tut - ta pie-tà _____

che si - i be-ne-det - ta, sei tut - ta pie-tà   Lil-let - ta

5 6   6   5♮6   6

_____ , son tut - ta pie-tà,   pie-

Lil-let - ta che si - i be -ne-det - ta, che si - i be - ne- det - ta, sei tut - ta pie-tà _____

6
5

54. Aria

55. Aria

131

So-no a-man-te d'un sem - bian-za,

so - no a-man-te d'un sem - bian-za che mi pia -cque, e che mi pia - ce,

che mi pia-cque e che mi pia - ce, mi pia-cque, mi pia-cque, mi pia - ce.

Van - ne sof - fri, e dat-ti pa - ce, e dat-ti pa -

ce.

56. Aria

me.

Vo - glio tan-to gi - rar-gli d'in-

[20]

-tor - no, gi - rar - - - - - - - - - -

(#6)

- - gli d'in -tor - no, fin-chè un gior - no pie - tà sen - ta del- le arse mie piu - me, sen - ta pie -

[25]

-tà, sen - ta pie-tà, del - le ar - - se mie piu - me. Far-fal-let - ta,

Dal segno

57 · Duetto

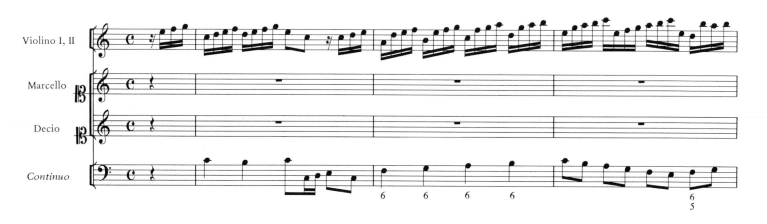

Violino I, II

Marcello

Decio

Continuo

6   6   6   6   6
                     5

134

58. Aria

138

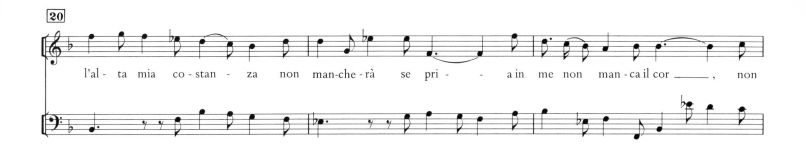

l'al - ta mia co - stan - za non man-che - rà se pri - - - a in me non man - ca il cor _____, non

man - - - - - - - - - - - - ca, non man - ca il cor.

Da capo

59. *Aria*

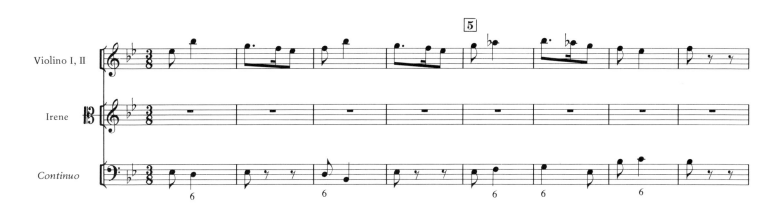

Violino I, II

Irene

Continuo

Più non vo - glio a - mar-ne tan - ti, vo-glio a - ma - re un vol - to sol,

tanti a - mar - ne più non vo - glio, voglio a - ma - re un vol - to sol,

voglio a - ma - re un vol - to sol.

Chè l'an - dar can - gian - do a - man - ti

è un can - giar duo - lo per duol, chè l'an - dar can - gian - do a - man - ti

è un can - giar duo - lo per duol, è un can - giar duo - lo per duol.

p

Da capo

60. *Arioso*

La tua sorte mi duole, mi duole più non gli pia - ci no, più non ti vuo - le, non ti vuo - le in - co - stan - te lu - sin - ghie - ra, can - gia co - re o can - gia, can - gia vol - to, menzo - gne - ra....

61. *Aria*

Se mai non è l'i - stesso quel ben che il cor de - si - a, non è, non è, l'i - stesso quel ben che il cor de - si - a è mia fa - ta - li - tà, è mia fa - ta - li - tà, è mia fa - ta - li - tà.

Co-me si can-gi spes-so la fiam-ma che m'ac-cenda quest' al-ma non l'inten-de, I - re-ne non lo sa, quest' al-ma non l'inten - de, I - re-ne non lo sa, non l'in - ten-de, non lo sa.

Dal segno

62. *Aria*

Violino I, II

Flavia

Que - gli oc - chi _____, o Dio, que-gli oc - chi,

Continuo

que-gli oc - chi _____, o Dio, que - gli oc - chi san da - re cer - ti sguar - di che e-

spri - me - re non so quan - to, quan - to ra - pi - sco-no; que-

63. Aria

144

64. Aria

Violino solo

Marcello

Bei lab - bri a - do - ra - ti di - re - te di sì, di sì, di sì, di -

Violoncello solo

[Senza cembalo]

re - te bei lab - bri a - do - ra - ti di sì, di sì di - re - te, di - re - te di

sì, sì, sì, di - re - te di sì.

f

f [Con cembalo]

Non sem - pre spie-

p

p [Senza cembalo]

7 6

6
5

ta - ti sa - re - te co - sì co - sì spie - ta - ti, non sem - pre spie - ta - ti sa-

re - te co - sì, spie - ta - ti non sem - pre sa - re - te co - sì.

Da capo

65. *Aria*

Que-ste pu-pil - le al - me -no vi -sce -re del mio se -no al - lor, al -

lor chiu-de - te, vi -sce -re del mio se -no, que -ste pu-pil - le al -me - no al-

lor chiu-de - te.   E al fred-do bu-sto ac-can - to,

10

tut-to can-gia-to in pian-to, il lat-te che vi die - di a me ren-de - te, a me ren-de - te.

Da capo

[66. *Quartetto* "Deh parla – Rispondi"]

67. Aria Buffa

Violino I, II

Livio

Continuo

68. Recitativo

Alfeo: (E' Lil - la, o non è Lil -la, for - se mi s'è ab-ba - glia - ta l'una, e l'al - tra pu-pil - la? E' Lil - la, o non è Lil - la?) (Ecco Al - feo, ci ho pur gu - sto.) Lil - la

Livio: per - chè non vai con ves -ta, e bu - sto? Che Lil - la? Con chi l'hai?

Alfeo: Se tu Lil - la non sei, ti ras-so-mi - gli tut - to quanto a le - i, e per la so - mi - glian - za che hai con la sua sem-bian-za, un ge -nio di gio-var-ti mi tra-spor-ta.

Livio: Giu - ro che non son Lil - la.

Alfeo: (E' molto, è molto accor -ta.) Perchè il Cie- lo ti fe si - mi-le a quel - la la tua for - tu - na in -vi - dio.

Pe - rò quel - la non son. Non da fa - sti - dio. Sap - pi ch'io son dot-

to - re. Pa - dron mio, ser - vi - to - re. A - vrai più vol - te in - te -so no - mi - na - re

il si - gnor don Al - fe - o. Sì sì mi pa - re. Sot - to di me che son pe - ri - to, e

sag - gio fa - re - sti ne - gli stud-ii un gran pas - sag - gio. Spie - ga - mi il tuo pen - sie - ro.

Io, per sco-prir-ti il ve - ro, mi di-let-to un tan - tin di po - e - si - a. Ma - le, ma-

- le. Per - chè? De - vi - a dagli al - tri studii, e ne - ce - sarii, e gra - vi. Per - chè son me-no

150

69. Duetto

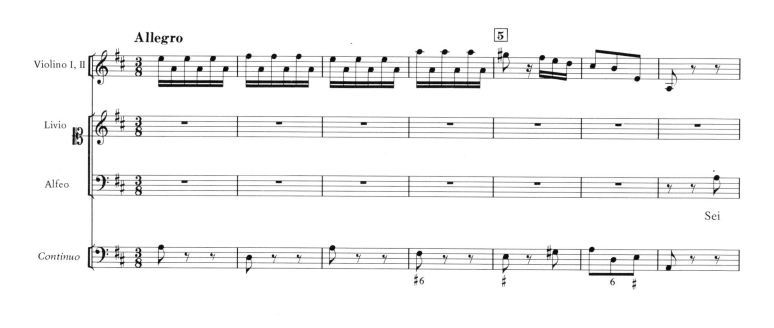

152

Da capo

71. *Ensemble*

1a volta: Marcello
2a, 3a volta: tutti

Continuo

Al - le

gio - ie, al - le gio-ie, bel-le a-nime a-man-ti che al-le gio-ie v'in-vi-ta l'a-mor, al - le gio-ie v'in-vi - ta l'a-mor.

Quel di - let-to che na-sce dai pian-ti è il di- let-to più dolce d'un cor, è il di - let-to più dol-ce d'un cor.

Da capo

APPENDIXES

A1. *Aria*

A2. *Aria*

tan - to è pri - va di pie - tà, quanto è bel - la tanto è pri - va di pie-

tà, quanto è bel - la tan - to è pri - va di pie - tà.

Io vor - rei tro - va-re in quel - la men ri - go - re, men ri - go - re

o men bel-tà, vor - rei tro-var in quel - la

men ri - go - re, men ri - go - re o men bel - tà o men bel -tà.

Da capo

A3. Aria

A4. *Aria*

pe -ne, pe -ne, pe-ne tro-van-do va, pe - ne, pe - ne, pe-ne tro-van-do va.

Non si so-spi - ra, non

si so-spi - ra un be - ne sen - za, sen-za ri-va-li-tà

non si sos-pi - ra un be - ne

sen - za, sen-za ri-va-li-tà, sen - za ri-va-li-tà. Chi

Dal segno

A5. *Duetto* [No. 69, *Br*]

più non di -rò   no   no   di - co di   no ti
sei Lil - la sei Lil - la sei Lil - la sei Lil - la sei   Lil - la

di - co di   no ti di - co di   no   di   no no no   no no no   no.
Lil - la   quel - la fa - vel - la

A6. Fragment from *Pn*, f. 96

A7. *Aria*

171

Appendix B.   Texts of Added or Substituted Numbers
in the Parma Libretto

Aria (Damiro)
I.ii (p. 15)

Luci vezzose addio.
Parto ma per tornare
A rimirare in voi quanto desio.
Luci vezzose addio.

Aria (Flavia)
II.vii (p. 54)

Sì, sì fedele
A te mio cor sarò:
E senza Irene,
Trà mille pene,
Forse Damiro un dì pianger vedrò.
Sì, sì, etc.

Aria (Decio)
II.ix (p. 59)
(Sustitute for No. 37)

Gran tormento del mio core,
Colla sferza del timore,
Cieco amore ti flagella.
E pur tutti ancor non sai,
Come dolce i vaghi rai
Volga ad altri la tua stella.
Gran, etc.

Quartet (Flavia, Irene, Damiro, Iliso)
II.xii (p. 62)
(Substitute for No. 44)

Begli occhi s'avvampo,
Esce l'incendio mio da un vostro
        lampo.
Le Stelle
Più belle
Non ardono in Cielo,
Ne il chiaro Dio di Delo
Strugge con tanti rai i fior nel campo.
Belgi occhi, etc.

Aria (Decio?)
III.i (p. 75)

Amorosi miei pensieri
Deh quietate i miei sospiri.
Dite al cor, che più non spera
Ne' fallaci suoi desiri.
Amorosi, etc.

Aria (Irene)
III.iii (p. 83)
(Substitute for No. 54)

Ah, che ritorni ancora
Nel centro del mio cor,
Mio caro, dolce amor,
Iliso amato!
Ovunque volga il guardo,
Se te non veggio, ond' ardo,
Si rende il mio dolor
Troppo spietato.
Ah, etc.

Aria (Iliso)
III.v (p. 84)

Vanne, che forse amore
Pietade avrà di me.
Difenda il Ciel clemente
Questo core innocente,
Tutto costanza, e fè.
Vanne, etc.

Aria (Iliso)
III.vii (p. 88)
(Compare No. 33)

Più non ti voglio nò: più non mi piaci.
Per ardere il mio cor
Amor, senti, per te non hà più faci.
Più, etc.

Aria (Irene)
III.viii (p. 89)
(Substitute for No. 61)

Spera; chi sà?
Forse si cangierà la fortuna un dì.
Credilo a me sì, sì ti sanerà
Lo stral che ti ferì.
       Spera, etc.

Aria (Damiro)
III.xv (p. 94)
(Substitute for No. 56)

Povero ruscelletto
Son' io d'amor per te.
Di tua bellezza al mare
Corr' io con onde chiare,
Senza fermar il piè.
Candido, puro, e schietto
Serbo nel cor la fè.

L'ERACLEA

DRAMA PER MUSICA
DI SILVIO STAMPIGLIA
TRA GLI ARCADI
PALEMONE LICURIO
DEDICATO

All'Illustriss. & Eccellentiss. Signora
LA SIGNORA

D. MARIA

DE GIRON, Y SANDOVAL
Ducheffa di Medina-Celi, e
Viceregina di Napoli.

IN NAPOLI 1700.
Per Dom. Ant. Parrino, e Michele Luigi Mutio,
Con Licenza de'Superiori.
Si vende nella Stampa del Mutio, fita
allo Spedaletto

NAPLES LIBRETTO

Facsimile / Translation

Mutazioni.

ATTO PRIMO.

Piccolo Tempio degli Dei Penati nel Palazzo d'Eraclea.

Palazzo d'Eraclea, e del Senato corrispondente al Porto di Siracusa.

ATTO SECONDO.

Sala apparata per solenne festino.

Deliziosa con cascate d'Acqua.

ATTO TERZO.

Mezzanini del Palazzo d'Eraclea.

Appartamenti nobili d'Eraclea.

Tempio degli Dei.

INTERMEDII.

I.

Di giochi di Picca, Bandiera, e Spada.

II.

Di forze diverse.

La Scena si finge in Siracusa.

Le Scene sono del Famoso Signor Ferdinando Galli detto Bibiena Ingegniero del Sereniss. di Parma.

A T-

ATTO PRIMO.

SCENA PRIMA.

Piccolo Tempio degli Dei Penati nel Palazzo d'Eraclea, al quale corrispondono per varie porte le Stanze dell'Appartamento della Medesima.

Eraclea, Irene, e Flavia che fuggono da molte genti armate, che vogliono ucciderle.

Decio, e Livio in habito da Donna, che tentano salvarle.

Er. Pietà.
Ir. Soccorso.
Fla. Aita.
Dec. Ah Tiranno. *trattenendo uno.*
Liv. Ah crudel. *trattenendo un altro*
Er. Amici, oh Dio
E in che peccammo, e le mie figlie ed io?
Dec Che tenti? *ad uno e vuol uccidere Irene.*
Liv. Che presumi? *ad un altro che vuol uccider Flavia.*
Er. O stelle.
Ir. O Cieli.
Fla. O Numi.
Er. Deh per mercede o bellicose squadre,
Vivan le figlie mie, mora la Madre.
Dec. Temerario che fai? *Disarma uno che vuol uccider Eraclea.*
Er Ferma Aldimira,
Cerca pietà non provocarli all'ira.
Ir. Eraclea.

A 6 Er.

ACT I

Scene i

Little temple of the Penates in Eraclea's palace, onto which the rooms of her apartment open through several doors; ERACLEA, IRENE, *and* FLAVIA, *fleeing from a large number of armed men who are intent on killing them;* DECIO *and* LIVIO, *in women's clothing, trying to save them.*

ER. Have pity!
IR. To the rescue!
FL. Help!
DEC. Oh, tyrant! *(holding one man back)*
LI. Oh, cruel one! *(holding another man back)*
ER. Friends, oh Heavens, what have we done wrong, my daughters and I?
DEC. What are you trying to do? *(to a man who is trying to kill* IRENE*)*
LI. What presumption is this? *(to another who is trying to kill* FLAVIA*)*
ER. O stars!
IR. O heavens!
FL. O Gods!
ER. Ah, have mercy, warlike troops, let my daughters live, let their mother die.
DEC. Rash man, what are you doing? *(disarms a man who is trying to kill* ERACLEA*)*
ER. Stop, Aldimira, beg for pity, do not provoke them to wrath.
IR. Eraclea!

a.Genitrice.
Er. Povera Irene mia, Flavia infelice.
  Ah fosse stato almeno
  Sterile questo seno,
  Non soffrireste voi sì dura forte,
  E me tormenteria solo una morte.
Dec. Ne pur v'impietosite?   *agl'armati.*
Ir. Son morta.
Fla. Ohime.
Liv. Che gran sventura !
Er. Udite.   *ai sudetti.*
  Già da spada inumana.
  Cadde la mia Germana al suol trafitta,
  E già di Siracusa.
  Trucidata da voi l'alta famiglia,
  Sparse d'atroce orror chiuse le ciglia ,
  E del Real mio sangue
  Ancor satii non siete?
  E non bastò più d'una vita esangue
  Del vostro sdegno a mitigar la sete?
  Se pur sì poco e tanto sangue, e tanto ,
  Eccovi il mio tutto stillato in pianto .
Dec. E nude ancor stan l'armi?
Ir. O fierezza .
Fla. O rigore.
Liv Ne in voi comincia a intenerirsi il core?
Er. Implacabili genti
  Se non vi movon queste
  Lagrime così meste ,
  Deh vi movano almen quelle innocenti.
Dec. Tu non morrai(cor mio)
  O se morrai, teco morir vogl'io.
Liv: Ah Signora fuggite .
vedendo che si movono i popoli per ucciderla , e
   vien difesa da Decio .
Dec. Inumani, che ardite?
  Barbari, che tentate?
D. Ah Madre.
      Fl.

Fla. Ah Madre mia.
Er. Figlie.

SCENA II.

Damiro, e detti .

Dam. FErmate, *si fermano i popoli armati.*
  Contro la Regia stirpe
De Sicani Tiranni
Bastan le fatte stragi,
Ogn'un riserbi a miglior uso il brando
Il Senato l'impose,io lo comando .
Itene al'alta impresa
De la nostra difesa ;
Mille Romane antenne
Sfidano a guerra noi, Marcello venne.
Dec. Olà prendi il tuo ferro.
    a quello a cui lo tolse.
Liv. E voi chetatevi.   *ad Irene, e Flavia.*
  Pigliate il fazzoletto, ed asciugatevi .
Ir. Mi consolo .
Fla. Respiro .
Er. A te gratie Damiro,
  E gratie a te,che generosa e forte, *a Dec.*
  Tanto sapesti noi scampar da morte.
Dam. O quanto vado altero
  D'aver sottratto a sanguinoso occaso ,
  Un Sol che diè due Stelle,
  Al Ciel d'Amor sì luminose, e belle.
Dec. E vò superba anch' io ,
  Perche in vita serbai
  La più degna beltà (l'Idolo mio)
Er. O voi scherzate meco,
  O tu sei lusinghiera,o tu sei cieco.
Ir. Che gentil Cavalier .
    tra loro guardano tutte due Damiro .
Fla. Che vaga Idea.
    Dam

FL. Mother!
ER. My poor Irene, unlucky Flavia! Ah, if this womb had at least been unfruitful, you would not suffer such a cruel fate, and only one death would be my torment.
DEC. Will you have no pity? (to the armed man)
IR. I'm done for!
FL. Woe is me!
LI. What great misfortune!
ER. Listen! (to the aforementioned)
My sister has already fallen pierced by an inhuman sword, and the ruling family of Syracuse has already closed its eyes, bloodied by atrocious horrors. Are you not yet sated with my royal blood? And has not more than one life, drained of its blood, been enough to slake the thirst of your hatred? If so much and yet again so much blood has not sufficed, here is mine, all dissolved in tears.
DEC. And are your weapons still unsheathed?
IR. O what fury!
FL. O what harshness!
LI. And do not your hearts begin to be softened?
ER. Pitiless people, if these tears of mine, so sad, do not affect you, ah, let these innocent tears move you.
DEC. You will not die, my heart, or if you die, I will die with you.
LI. Oh, madame, flee! (seeing that the mob is moving to kill her and that she is defended by DECIO)
DEC. Inhuman one, what are you daring to do? Barbarians, what are you attempting?
IR. Oh, Mother!

FL. Oh, my mother!
ER. My daughters!

Scene ii
DAMIRO *and the foregoing*

DAM. Stop! (*The armed men desist.*) The executions that have already been carried out against the royal family of the tyrants of Sicily are enough. Let everyone keep his sword for a better use. The Senate has decreed it. I order it. Go the noble task of our defense. A thousand Roman masts are challenging us to battle. Marcello has come!
DEC. Hey, you! Take your sword (*to the man from whom he took it*).
LI. And you, calm down. Take this handkerchief and dry your tears.
IR. I am consoled.
FL. I breathe again.
ER. To you, Damiro, thanks. And (*to* DECIO) thanks to you who, noble and strong, were so skillful in saving us from death.
DAM. Oh, how proud I am to have saved, from a bloody death, a sun which gave the heaven of Love two such bright and beautiful stars.
DEC. And I, too, am proud to have kept alive the most exalted beauty (my idol!).
ER. Either you are joking with me, or you (*to* DECIO) are flattering me, or you (*to* DAMIRO) are blind.
IR. What a noble knight!   ⎫
FL. What a fair ideal!   ⎬ (*both look at* DAMIRO)

Dam. Belliffima Eraclea
    Alta cura di ftato
    A Configlio mi chiama, e preffo è l'ora.
Ir. Egli a me piace.   *come fepra.*
Jla. Ed a me piace ancora.
Dam. Se contenta tu fei partir defio.
Er. Damiro và.
    Dam. s'incbina ad Eraclea poi dice pian.à
         Fla. & ad Irene .
Dam. Luci vezzofe addio .   *parte.*
Ir. Diffe a le mie o a lè pupille tue ?
Fl. A chi diffe non sò .
Liv. Egli ai lumi parlò di tutte due.
Er. Irene, Flavia mia,
    Del paffato periglio
    Di noftra forte eftrema
    E fvanita da voi tutta la tema ?
Fla.   Ancora il fen mi palpita.
Ir.   Ancor mi batte il cor.
Fla.   Mi par che fia queft'alma
    Non ben tornata in calma .
Ir.   E queffo feno ingombra
    Qualch'ombra
    Di timor.
Fla.   Ancora il fen mi palpita.
Ir.   Ancor mi batte il cor .

S C E N A   III.

Eraclea , Decio , e Livio .

Si guardano attentamente Eraclea, e Decio.
Liv. FRena Sig. l'occhiate.   *piano à Decio.*
    Và più cauto, e più faggio ,
    Che fi verrà a fapere,
    Che tù fei Cavaliere, e ch'io fon paggio.
Dec. Lilla parti .
Liv. Obedifco .   *parte.*
          Dec.

Dec. Scufa Eraclea fe ardifco ;
    E perche mai così mi guardi attenta?
Er. Rifletto al tuo coraggio
    Scorgo che Donna fei,
    E reftano confufi i penfier miei.
Dec. A prò de la tua vita
    Diè lena il Cielo a quefto braccio imbelle,
    La virtù non fù mia fù de le Stelle.
Er. E degno il tuo valore
    D'alta mercè, chiedi che brami.
Dec. Amore.
Er. Viver certa ne puoi.
Dec. C ò farà vero?
Er. Credimi.
Dec. Non lo fpero.
Er. Se temi, temi in vano.
Dec. Me'l giuri ?
Er. Ecco la deftra.
Dec. (O cara mano)
    Ma s'io non foffi, oh Dio....
    (Scoprirmi è forza)
Er. Spiegati.
Dec. Pavento .
Er. Perche ?
Dec. Perche fon rea
    D'alto ardimento.
Er. Io del ardir t'affolvo,
    E fa qual mi figura un mio penfiero
    Anche un vomo tù foffi, io ti perdono .
Dec. Non t'ingana il pefier, che Decio io fono
Er. Quel che al Volturno in riva
    Traffe i natali fuoi Decio ai Romani
    Si coftante e fedel?
Dec. Quello .
Er. Che afcolto !
    Chi ti fè mentir feffo ?
Dec. Il tuo bel volto.
Er. E quando, e come, e dove?
          Dec.

DAM. Most beautiful Eraclea, the exalted cares of state call me to council, and the hour is at hand.

IR. I am attracted to him.

FL. And I too am attracted to him. } (*as above*)

DAM. If you are willing, I desire to take my leave.

ER. Go, Damiro.

(*Damiro bows to Eraclea, then says sotto voce to Flavia and Irene:*)

DAM. Charming eyes, farewell.

IR. Was he speaking to my eyes or yours?

FL. I don't know who he was talking to.

LI. He was talking to the eyes of both of you.

ER. My Irene, my Flavia, has all the terror of the danger we have passed through, of our extreme peril, left you?

FL. My bosom is still heaving.

IR. My heart is still pounding.

FL. It seems to me that this spirit has not yet calmed down.

IR. And this bosom is still oppressed by some shadow of fear.

FL. My bosom is still heaving.

IR. My heart is still pounding.

Scene iii
ERACLEA, DECIO, *and* LIVIO

(ERACLEA *and* DECIO *look attentively at each other.*)

LI. (*Sotto voce to* DECIO) Restrain your glances, my lord. Be more careful and cautious, for otherwise it will become known that you are a knight and I am a page boy.

DEC. Lilla, leave us.

LI. At your orders. (*Exit.*)

DEC. Forgive me, Eraclea, if I am so bold: why do you look so attentively at me?

ER. I am thinking of your courage. I realize that you are a woman, and my thoughts are confused.

DEC. To save your life, Heaven gave strength to this weak arm. The power was not mine, but of the stars.

ER. Your bravery deserves an exalted reward. Ask what you will.

DEC. Love.

ER. You can be certain of it.

DEC. Can this be true?

ER. Believe me.

DEC. I do not hope for it.

ER. If you fear, you fear in vain.

DEC. Do you swear it to me?

ER. Here is my right hand.

DEC. (O beloved hand!) But if I were not, O Heaven . . . (I must disclose my identity.)

ER. Explain yourself.

DEC. I am afraid.

ER. Why?

DEC. Because I am guilty of excessive daring.

ER. I pardon you for your daring; and know what a notion of mine suggests to me: even if you were a man, I forgive you.

DEC. Your notion does not deceive you, for I am Decio.

ER. That Decio who was born on the banks of the Volturnus, and who was so loyal and faithful to the Romans?

DEC. The same.

ER. What do I hear! What made you conceal your sex?

DEC. Your fair countenance.

ER. When, and how, and where?

Dec. Pria di mirarti io per te piansi altrove,
   E su 'e da la Patria
   Scherzo del mare irato,
   Salvo portommi in Aleſſandria il fato.
Er. Dimmi là conoſceſti
   L'eſtinto mio conſorte?
Dec. Stretta amiſtà ſempre paſsò tra noi
   Sin ch'hebbe ai giorni ſuoi ſera di morte;
   Egli tal'or meco lodar ſolea
   Più de la tua ſembianza
   La bell'anima tua.
Er. Che rimembranza!   *ſi mette a piangere*
Dec. Onde de tuoi coſtumi
   Al'or m'acceſi, ed arſi,
   E ſallo amor quanti ſoſpiri hò ſparſi.
   Eraclea perche piangi ?
   Mentre ti ſciogli in lagrimoſi rivi,
   Moſtri pietade ai morti, e uccidi *i vivi.*
   Ah che di ſtille amare
   Le belle gote inutilmente aſpergi ,
   Deh conſolati, e tergi
   L'umide ciglia, ed a me dona un guardo,
   A me che già tutt' ardo
   Di puro foco oneſto.
   Senti ben mio.
Er. (Che Laberinto è queſto!)   *ſta penſoſa.*
Dec. Non cangiai nome , e ſpoglia
   Per far oltraggio al tuo pudico onore,
   Ma con limpida voglia
   Di ſervir te per meritarne amore; (preſti
   Se queſto è ardir che ſdegno al cor t' ap-
   Ricordati Eraclea , che m'aſſolveſti .
   Ed ancor sì penſoſa?
Er. (Sto pur dubioſa!
   Che far non sò)
Dec. Riſpondi alma adorata.
Er. (Tutta agitata
   Io mi confondo,

   E non riſpondo,
   Ne sì, ne nò.
   Sto pur, &c.
Dec. Pietà , pietà mio bene,
   Ti movan le mie pene,
   La libertà perduta ,
   Il mio cor lacerato. E ancor ſtai muta?
   Eraclea volgi almeno
   Per dar pace al mio ſeno,
   De la chiara tua fronte a me le faci,
   Mio cor, mia vita.
Er. Amami, ſervi, e taci.
Dec. Saprò pupille care ,
   Saprò ſerbare amore,
   Silentio , e ſervitù;
   Come ſaprà il mio core
   Servir , tacere, e amare
   Lo ſcorgerai ben tù .
   Saprò, &c.

S C E N A   IV.

Eraclea.

AH Decio Decio a farmi guerra al'alma
   E qual deſtin t'hà moſſo?
Condennar ti vorrei, ma poi non poſſo.
Confuſa la ragione,
Vede che hà poſto amore
Stretto aſſedio al mio core, e nol difende,
Ma patteggia con lui, cede , e ſi rende.
   Io ſento un non sò chè ,
   Che in petto a poco a poco
   Và diventando foco,
   E il cor m'accende ;
   Io non sò dir com'è,
   Queſto naſcente ardor ,
   Ma chi conoſce amor
   Sò

DEC. Before seeing you, I wept for you elsewhere. As an exile from my native land, a plaything of the angry sea, I was carried by Fate safe to Alexandria.

ER. Tell me, did you know my late husband there?

DEC. There was always a close friendship between us, until death brought the evening of his days; and Cupid alone knows how many sighs I have cast on the air. Eraclea, why are you weeping? When you are dissolved in rivers of tears, you are showing pity to the dead and are killing the living. Oh, you are fruitlessly bedewing your fair cheeks with bitter tears. Ah, console yourself, wipe your damp eyes, and grant me a glance—me, who am already all afire with a pure, honorable flame. Listen to me, my beloved.

ER. What a labyrinth is this! *(remains lost in thought)*

DEC. I did not change my name and garb in order to outrage your modesty and honor, but did so out of a pure desire to serve you and to deserve your love thereby. If this is boldness which brings disdain to your heart, remember, Eraclea, that you have already pardoned me. Are you still so thoughtful?

ER. (I am still hesitant! I do not know what to do.)

DEC. Answer me, beloved heart.

ER. (I am all upset and confused, and I can answer neither yes nor no. I am still, etc.)

DEC. Have pity, have pity, my beloved. Let my sufferings, my lost freedom, my wounded heart move you to pity. Are you still silent? Eraclea, at least turn the torches of your shining brow toward me, to give peace to my bosom, O my heart, my life.

ER. Love me, serve me, and be silent.

DEC. I shall know, O beloved eyes, how to keep love and silence and service. How my heart will be able to serve, be silent, and love, you will clearly see. I shall know, etc.

Scene iv
ERACLEA

Ah, Decio, Decio, what fate moved you to make war on my heart? I would like to blame you, but I cannot. With my reason awhirl, I see that Love has laid a close siege to my heart, and is not defending it, but is making a treaty with him and is surrendering it.

I feel a certain something in my bosom, which is gradually turning into a fire and is setting my heart ablaze. I cannot tell what it is like, this burgeoning flame, but I know that anyone who is acquainted with love under-

Sò che m'intende .
Io sento, &c.

SCENA V.

Flavia, Irene, Alfeo, e Livio.

Al. MIe difcepole vaghe ,
    Avvertite che amore
Incurabili al core apre le piaghe .
Ir. Se con puro defio
    Io foffi amante?
Fla. E foffi amante anch'io?
Al. Lodo l'amore onefto,
    Ma bifogna andar caute ancor con quefto.
    Speffo con falfe imagini
    Apparir fà innocente un penfier reo .
Li. Le folite feccagini
    Signor Dottore Alfeo .
Al. Taci Lilla (è pur bella)
Li Io non voglio tacere .
Al. E tù favella.
Ir. Dunque dentro al mio core.
Fla. Dunque dentro al mio petto.
Ir. Poffo nudrire un bel intatto amore?
Fa. Poffo ferbare un bel pudico affetto ?
Al. E varia l'opinione,
    Molti dicon di sì, molti di nò.
Li. Ci vvol rifolutione ,
    Si può dargli ricetto, o non fi può?
Al. Bifogna con giuditio
    Fuggir fempre il periglio,
    (Che bocca oh dio, che ciglio,
                  guardando Lilla.
    Alfeo Alfeo ftà faldo)
    Amore hà un brutto vitio
    D'avvelenar lo ftrale,
    (In fomma l'uomo è frale,
                       Mi

Mi fento venir caldo). *come fopra.*
Bifogna, &c.

SCENA VI.

Irene, Flavia, e Livio.

Li. MI pare troppo ftitico
    Quel voftro Signor cofo,
Nol vorrei sì politico ,
Ne tanto fcrupolofo,
Lafciatelo ciarlare .
Più ragazze non fiete ,
Ma il tempo avete in cui fi deve amare .
Ir. Amo .
Fl. Ed amo ancor'io.
Ir. Damiro è il mio bel fol.
Fl. Damiro è il mio.
Li. Come? un folo è l'oggetto,
    Che il voftro cor defia ?
   Ne c'entra gelofia?
Ir. La gelofia cos'è?
Fl. In van lo chiedi a me.
Ir. Che? nemen tù lo fai?
Fl. Non sò che fia, ne la conobbi mai.
Li. E meglio ftarne fenza.
Ir. Lo farò .
Fl. Te'l prometto .
Li. (O che innocenza.)
Ir. Lilla più volte hò intefo,
    Che un amante fi more,
    Mi fpiaceria, che daffe morte amore.
Li. Dà morte, ma una morte,
    Che di dolce piacer l'anime pafce,
    Perche un amante core,
    E tofto more, e tofto poi rinafce.
Fl. Io per amor non fono morta ancora,
    Ma goderei provar come fi mora .
                       Non

---

stands me. I feel, etc.

Scene v
FLAVIA, IRENE, ALFEO, *and* LIVIO

AL. My dear pupils, take note that love opens incurable wounds in the heart.

IR. But if I loved with a pure desire?

FL. And if I were in love too?

AL. I praise honorable love, but you must be careful with it, too. Often it makes an evil thought appear innocent, with deceitful imaginings.

LI. Your usual boring tommyrot, Doctor Alfeo.

AL. Quiet, Lilla. (She *is* beautiful!)

LI. I won't keep quiet.

AL. And you, speak.

IR. So, in my heart . . .

FL. So, in my bosom . . .

IR. . . . can I nourish a beautiful, pure love?

FL. . . . can I harbor a beautiful, modest affection?

AL. Opinions vary. Some say yes, others no.

LI. Make up your mind. Can one allow it or not?

AL. One must always wisely flee danger. (What a mouth, oh God, what eyelashes!) (*Looking at* LILLA:) (Alfeo, Alfeo, stand firm!) Love has a bad habit of poisoning his arrows. (In short, man is weak. I feel I am getting hot.) One must always, etc.

Scene vi
IRENE, FLAVIA, *and* LIVIO

LI. That Mr. Whoozis of yours seems to me too costive. I would not like him to be so politic, nor so finicky. Let him chatter; you are no longer girls, but are at the time in which you should love.

IR. I am in love.

FL. I, too, am in love.

IR. Damiro is my beautiful sun.

FL. Damiro is mine.

LI. What? Is there only one object of your love, that the hearts of both of you desire? And does not jealousy come into the picture?

IR. What is jealousy?

FL. No use asking me.

IR. What? Don't you know, either?

FL. I have no idea what it is, nor have I ever known it.

LI. It's better to get along without it.

IR. I shall do so.

FL. I promise you.

LI. (Oh, what innocence!)

IR. Lilla, I've often heard tell that a lover dies. I'd be sorry for love to cause death.

LI. It causes death, but a death which feeds souls with sweet delight, because a loving heart quickly dies and then is quickly reborn.

FL. I have not yet died for love, but I should like to find out how one dies.

Non voglio gelofia ,
    Ma folo voglio amor ;
    E al alma piaceria,
    Che m'uccideffe ogn'or.
Non, &c.

S C E N A VII.

Irene , e Livio .

Li. SCufi la confidenza ,
    Ilifo tuo fe sà,
Quefto novello amor,che mai dirà?
Ir. Dica pur ciò che vvole ;
    Che forfe non pofs'io
Andar cangiando amore a voler mio?
Li. Così prefto ti fciogli ?
Ir. Mai legata non fui .
Li. E lafci Ilifo, e già Damiro accogli?
Ir. E Ilifo lafci me s'io lafcio lui.
Li. Irene a quel che fento
    Ti ferve amore di trattenimento;
    Con fomma cortefia
    Non ti dà gelofia,non t'incatena.
Ir. Amo per mio piacer, non per mia pena.
    E un amor che alletta poco
    L'amar fempre due pupille;
    Io che amando amo per gioco,
    Voglio amarne, e cento , e mille.
    E un, &c.

S C E N A VIII.

Livio .

CErto, chi lo può fare ,
    Amar per fvario è un gufto fingolare;
Mà è gufto affai maggiore
Effer creduto Donna, ed effer uomo ,
               Par-

Pratico à tutte l'ore
Con due Regie Donzelle ,
La difcorra con quelle ,
Mà fempre vò col debito rifpetto ;
Povero Giovanetto
Io fono è ver, mà non hò cor plebeo .
Solo tal'or però
In bagatelle dò con Don Alfeo.
    E pur ftrano veder con la gonna
       Un Ragazzo, che faccia da Donna,
       Strafcinare tre palmi di coda .
       Mi conviene fapermi inchinare
       Far più fmorfie,con gratia fputare,
       E ballare fecondo la moda .
    E pur ftrano, &c.

S C E N A IX.

*Palazzo d'Eraclea,e del Senato,che corri-
fponde al Porto di Siracufa.
Marcello che sbarca nel Porto di Siracufa con
numerofo feguito .
Damiro , e Ilifo da una parte , che fcendono
dalle fcale del Palazzo del Senato .
Decio, Eraclea, Flavia, ed Irene dall' altra ,
che fcendono dalle Scale del Real
Palazzo .*

Mar. S Piegan fempre le Navi Latine
    Belle vele d'amica fortuna ,
    Che le guida col biondo fuo crine
    Dove il fato gran prede l'aduna.
    Spiegan, &c.
Dam. Ecco invtto Marcello,
    Che viene Siracufa
      gli prefenta una corona d'alloro.
    Ad offrir degni lauri à la tua chioma,
    E la Real Cervice inchina à Roma .
Il. De'conquiftati allori

I don't want jealousy, I want only love; and it would please my soul, if it were to kill me every hour. I don't want, etc.

Scene vii
IRENE *and* LIVIO

LI. Excuse my forwardness: if your Iliso finds out about this new love of yours, what will he say?

IR. Let him say anything he wants to. Perhaps I can't change my love as I see fit?

LI. Do you detach yourself so quickly?

IR. I was never attached.

LI. And you desert Iliso and already receive Damiro into your heart?

IR. Then let Iliso desert me, if I desert him.

LI. Irene, so far as I can see, love is just an amusement for you. With all due respect, it does not cause you jealousy nor enchain you.

IR. I love for my pleasure, not for my pain.
It is a love which delights but little, that which always loves only two eyes. I, who, when loving, love for fun, want to love a hundred and a thousand. It is a love, etc.

Scene viii
LIVIO

Certainly, for anyone who can, loving for amusement is a singular taste. I find it much more fun to be thought a woman and to be a man. I frequent two royal damsels all the time and talk with them, but I always behave with due respect. I am a poor young man, it's true, but I have not got a plebeian heart. Only from time to time, however, I play the fool with Sir Alfeo.
It is indeed strange to see a boy acting like a girl, dragging three palm's lengths of train; I have to know how to curtsey, to make a lot of grimaces, to spit gracefully, and to dance according to the latest fashion. It is indeed strange, etc.

Scene ix
Palaces of ERACLEA *and the Senate, giving on the port of Syracuse;* MARCELLO, *disembarking in the port of Syracuse, with a large retinue;* DAMIRO *and* ILISO *on one side, descending from the steps of the Senate palace;* DECIO, ERACLEA, FLAVIA, *and* IRENE *on the other side, coming down from the steps of the royal palace.*

MAR. The ships of Rome always unfurl their sails to friendly Fortune, who guides them with her blond hair to where Fate brings together great booty for them. The ships of Rome unfurl, etc.

DAM. Behold, unconquered Marcello, Syracuse comes (*offers him a laurel crown*) to offer worthy laurels for your head, and bends her royal neck to Rome.

IL. You should, sir, encircle your brow with the laurels

Signor, la fronte tua cinger tu dei,
Che del'Aquile invitte il Giove fei.
Mar. Il tuo voler s'adempia,
E la mia man circondi
Del'onorate frondi à me le tempia
*Si mette la Corona d' Alloro à fuon
di Trombe.*
Quefta illuftre Ghirlanda
Più di voi,che di me ie glorie moftra,
Che il pefo è mio,mà la corona è voftra
*Fla.*Campion del Tebro e generofo,e forte
Eccone ai piedi tuoi.
Ir. Altri non fiamo noi,
Che avanzi miferabili di morte
Er. Quefte del feno mio
Son dolci parti,ed Eraclea fon'io.
Mar. Sorgete ; Inclita Donna
È chiaro in ogni lido
Di tua beltà di tua virtude il grido,
Ma in vagheggiare i lumi
Del tuo fembiante altero,
Trovo la fama affai minor del vero.
Er. Venne fu gl'occhi tuoi
La pietà che per me ti nacque in feno,
E guardandomi quella,
Il mio dolor fa ch'io ti fembri bella.
Mar. Se raffereni il ciglio,
Qual petto ai lampi tuoi fia che refifta,
Se tanto accendi, e lacrimofa,e trifta ?
Dec. Egli parla d'amore, *piano ad Erat.*
E fe pietofa al'amor fuo compiaci
Oh Dio fon morto.
Er. Amami,fervi, e taci. *pian.a Dec.*
Mar. (Già peno,già fofpiro.)
Marc. fempre guarda Eracl.
Fl. (Caro Damiro mio.)
Ir. (Caro Damiro)
Dam. (Irene anima mia)

Era-

*Eraclea e Decio con atti muti parlano
tra loro.*
Il. (Irene a me non bada,o gelofia)
Fl. Tutto languido in vifo
Ti va mirando Ilifo
Fla.& Irene piano tra loro.
Ir. A me che importa ?
Irene guarda Damiro.
Il. (Ah che tradito io fono)
Fl. Per pietà lo conforta. *piano come fopra.*
Ir. Io l'abbandono.
Dam. (Che leggiadra beltà) *guarda Irene.*
Mar. (Che nobil volto.) *guardando Eral.*
Er. Decio non paventar.
Eraclea, e Decio piano tra loro.
Dec. Ti guarda molto.
Mar. Ditemi chi è colei? *accennnndo a Dec.*
Il. Nobil ftraniera è quella .
Dam. Aldimira fi chiama.
Er. Ed è mia Dama.
Dec. Anzi fedele ancella.
Mar. Invidio la tua forte,
Dec. Non è ingiufta l'invidia .
*In quefto mentre Irene faluta fortivamente
Damiro.*
Il. (O con qual arti ,
Io mi veggio fchernir)
Mar.torna a guardare attentamentr Erac.
Dec. Torna a guardarti. *piano ad Erac.*
Mar. (Che maeftà che brio,
Che luminofe faci)
Dec. Non mi tradir ben mio.
piano tra loro .
Er. Amami, fervi, e taci.
Fla. (Che vaghe labra amene)
guardando tutte due Dam .
Ir. (Che dolci rai vivaci)
Il. (Ingannatrice Irene)

Dam.

---

you have won, for you are the Jove of the unconquered eagles.

MAR. Let your wish be fulfilled and let my hand encircle my brow with these honored leaves (*putting
on the laurel wreath to the sound of trumpets*). This
illustrious garland shows more your glory than
mine, for the burden is mine, but the glory is yours.

FL. O champion of the Tiber, noble and strong, behold
us at your feet.

IR. We are nothing but miserable relics of death.

ER. These girls are my beloved offspring, and I am
Eraclea.

MAR. Arise, renowned lady. The reputation of your
beauty and virtue is bright on every shore. But, on
admiring the glow of your exalted countenance, I
find the reputation greatly inferior to the truth.

ER. The pity for me which was born in your bosom
has risen into your eyes, and when it beheld me, my
sorrow made me seem beautiful to you.

MAR. Let your brow clear again. What bosom can resist your lightning bolts, if you kindle such a flame
when you are tearful and sad?

DEC. He is speaking of love (*sotto voce to* ERACLEA),
and if you look with pity and favor on his love, oh
Heavens, I am done for.

ER. Love me, serve me, and be silent (*sotto voce to*
DECIO).

MAR. (I am already tormented and sighing.) (MARCELLO
keeps his glance fixed on ERACLEA.)

FL. (My beloved Damiro!)

IR. (Damiro, my beloved!)

DAM. (Irene, my soul!)

(ERACLEA *and* DECIO *speak to each other in dumb show.*)

IL. (Irene pays no attention to me; O jealousy!)

FL. Iliso, with yearning in his face, is looking at you.

(FLAVIA *and* IRENE *converse sotto voce.*)

IR. What do I care?

IL. (Ah, I am betrayed!)

FL. For pity's sake, comfort him! (*sotto voce as above*)

IR. I care nothing for him.

DAM. (What fair beauty!) (*looks at* IRENE)

MAR. (What a noble face!) (*looks at* ERACLEA)

DEC. He is looking very hard at you.

MAR. Tell me, who is she? (*indicating* DECIO)

IL. She is a noble foreigner.

DAM. Her name is Aldimira.

ER. And she is my lady-in-waiting.

DEC. Nay, more, I am your faithful servant.

MAR. I envy you your good fortune.

DEC. Your envy is not ill founded.

(Meanwhile, IRENE *makes furtive signs to* DAMIRO.)

IL. Oh, with what wiles I see myself scorned.

(MARCELLO *again looks attentively at* ERACLEA.)

MAR. (What majesty, what life, what brilliant eyes!)

DEC. Do not betray me, my beloved. } (DECIO and
ER. Love me, serve me, and be silent. } ERACLEA converse
} sotto voce.)

FL. (What attractive, beautiful lips!) } (FLAVIA and
IR. (What sweet, lively eyes!) } IRENE both look
} at DAMIRO.)

Dam. (Quanto co●mio mi piaci.)

                   guard. Irene.

Che, &c.

S C E N A X.

Alfeo, e Livio.

Alf. O Perigliofo incontro:
    Deh ramentati Alfeo,
Che tu fei d'anni, e di giuditio carico.
Liv. M'inchino.
Alf. Addio (fe refto quì prevarico.)
Liv. Dunque tu vuoi lafciarmi?
    Pazienza, fei Padrone,
    E' però crudeltà.
Alf. (Che tentatione)
    Ah.
Liv. Perche fofpirate?
Alf. Andate Lilla andate.
    Oh.
Liv. Che mal vi fentite?
Alf. Lilla Lilla partite.
Liv. Ch'io parta? fervirollo,
    E però tirannia.
Alf. (Che rompicollo.)
    Uh.
Liv. Ma che cofa havete?
Alf. Lilla retrocedete.
Liv. Alfeo, che mai t'hò fatto,
         Lo vuol pigliare per mano
    Che mi fcacci così?
Alf. Piano col tatto.
Liv. Povere mie carezze
    Mal gradite da te.
Alf. (Che tenerezze.)
Liv. Son Donzelletta amabile,
    E fon concupifcibile
                      Son

    Son fvelta mà palpabile
    Son nubile, fon abile
    Ergo fon appetibile.
  Son, &c.
Alf. (O che impulfi, ò che guai.)
Liv. E dove troverai
    Una fpofetta oh Dio,
    Amorofa così, come fon'io?
    Per te di pianto afpergo
    L'uno e l'altro mio ciglio.
Alf. (Oh Dio quel ergo.)
Liv. Deh penfa a cafi tuoi;
    Se contrarre non vvoi quefti Imenei,
    Si perderà la razza degl'Alfei.
Alf. (Senfo fenfo ribaldo,
    Più non poffo ftar' faldo.)
Liv. E mi vorrai vedere
    Mefta così?
Alf. (Non poffo più tenere;)
    Io tengo tengo
    Ma più non poffo;
    Già me ne vengo,
    Alfeo s'è moffo.
  Io, &c.
Liv. Mia gioja, mio defire.
Alf. Non più, non più, che tu mi fai morire.
Liv. In te fol mi ricreo.
Alf. (Non ftare abbandonato animo Alfeo.)
    Mi fento ardito.
Liv.   (S'è rimbambito)
Alf.   Tutto mi fcuoto.
Liv.   (S'è meffo in moto.)
Alf.   Mio ben che fate?
Liv.   Non v'agitate
    Per carità.
Alf.   Tutta fpecifica,
    Mi revivifica
    La tua beltà.

                 B   Li.

IL. (Deceitful Irene!)

DAM. (How much I love you, dear heart!)   *(looking at* IRENE*)*

    What majesty, etc.

Scene x
ALFEO *and* LIVIO

AL. Oh, what a dangerous meeting! Ah, remember, Alfeo, you are weighted down with years and wisdom.

LI. My obeisances.

AL. Farewell. (If I remain here, I shall go astray.)

LI. So you want to leave me? All right, you can do as you wish, but this is cruelty nevertheless.

AL. (What a temptation!) Ah!

LI. Why are you sighing?

AL. Go away, Lilla, go away. Oh!

LI. Are you feeling bad?

AL. Lilla, Lilla, go away.

LI. I should go away? I will obey you—but this is tyranny, nevertheless.

AL. (What a mess!) Oh!

LI. But what's the matter with you?

AL. Lilla, go off.

LI. Alfeo, what harm have I done you *(tries to take his hand)* that you are chasing me away like this?

AL. Don't touch me.

LI. Poor caresses of mine, which displease you!

AL. (What tenderness!)

LI. I am a loveable and desirable damsel. I am slender but touchable. I am marriageable and clever, *ergo*, I am appetizing. I am, etc.

AL. Oh what impulses, oh what troubles!

LI. And where will you find a little bride, oh Heavens, as loving as I am? I am bedewing both my eyelashes with weeping for you.

AL. Oh Heavens, that *ergo!*

LI. Ah, think of your situation! If you don't want to enter on this marriage, the Alfeo family will die out.

AL. (Treacherous senses, I cannot be firm any longer!)

LI. And do you want to see me sad like this?

AL. (I can't resist any longer.)
I am resisting, resisting, but I can't any longer. I am already coming; Alfeo has gotten under way. I am resisting, etc.

LI. My joy, my desire.

AL. No more, no more, for you are making me die.

LI. My only joy is in you.

AL. (Don't give up; courage, Alfeo!)
I feel bold.

LI. (He is in his second childhood.)

AL. I am shaking all over.

LI. He has gotten under way.

AL. My dear, what are you doing?

LI. Don't get excited, for Heaven's sake.

AL. Quite specifically, your beauty revives me.

Liv. Signor Magnifico
Te la facrifico
Tal quale ftà .
Mi fento, &c.

S C E N A XI.

Flavia, e Damiro.

Fl. DAmiro .
Dam.   Flavia .
Fl. Uditti,
   Che fei l'Idolo mio ;
   Ora fe m'ami tù, faper defio.
Dam. E chi fdegnar può mai
   Te che fei degna tanto?
Fl. Col rifpondēr che fai
   Meco à nulla t'impegni ,
   Se m'ami io vvò faper, non fe mi fdegni.
Dam. Non ardifce il penfiero
   D'avvicinarfi al Sol .
Fl. No, dimmi il vero
   Ne paventar d'effer creduto audace.
Dam. Bella, fia con tua pace,
   E fe t'offendo hai da incolpar gli Dei ,
   Se diceffi d'amarti io mentirei?
Fl. E perche tù non m'ami?
Dam. Chiedilo agl'aftri.
Fl. Oh Dio,
   Chiedere agl' aftri ciò come pofs'io ?
Dam. Ah forfe non t'è noto .
   Ch'ha d'ogn'altro deftin forza maggiore ,
   Quello a cui diamo noi nome d'amore?
Fl. Potrei fapere almeno,
   Se t'hanno accefo altre pupille il feno ?
Dam. Nol niego, io fono amante .
Fl. Palefami la bella
   Da cui fofti rapito.

             Dam.

Dam. Irene è quella .
Fl. Non potrefti o mio bene,
   Amare a un tempo ifteffo, e Flavia, e Irene?
Dam. Nò, Flavia , nò che in quefto doppio
   Ti farei traditore.   (amore,
Fl. Ah Damiro Damiro,
   Solo d'Irene la beltà t'appaga,
   E Flavia agl'occhi tuoi non fembra vaga.
Dam. Io non dico che tu non fei bella ,
   Dico fol che deftino l'amore,
   Non è il genio, ch'è forza di ftella.
   Ed a quella foggiace ogni core.
Io, &c.

S C E N A XII.

Flavia .

O Qual nel petto mio
   Gronda gelida brina ,
Che fi và condenfando intorno al core,
E m'empie d'un infolito dolore.
   A quefto novo affanno
     Tutta s'abbandonò
     L'anima mia ,
     Tormento sì tiranno ,
     Altro effere non può,
     Che gelofia .
A quefto, &c.

S C E N A XIII.

Irene, e Ilifo.

Il. INgratiffima Irene ,
   E a chi per te ftà in pene
Negafti dar conforto
Con un tuo fguardo fol ?
         B 2   Ir.

LI. Magnificent sir, I sacrifice it all to you, just as it is. I feel, etc.

Scene xi
FLAVIA *and* DAMIRO

FL. Damiro!

DAM. Flavia!

FL. You have heard that you are my idol. Now I want to know if you love me.

DAM. And who can ever disdain you, who are so worthy?

FL. With the answer you give me, you are not committing yourself to me in any way. I want to know whether you love me, not whether you disdain me.

DAM. My thoughts do not dare to come near the sun.

FL. No, tell me the truth; do not be afraid of being thought bold.

DAM. My fair lady, by your leave—and if I offend you, you must blame the Gods—if I said I loved you, I would be lying.

FL. And why do you not love me?

DAM. Ask the stars.

FL. Oh heavens, how can I ask that of the stars?

DAM. Ah, perhaps you do not know that what we call love has a power greater than any other fate?

FL. Might I at least know whether other eyes have enkindled your bosom?

DAM. I do not deny it, I am in love.

FL. Tell me who is the beauty by whom you were captured.

DAM. It is Irene.

FL. Could you not, O my beloved, love both Flavia and Irene at the same time?

DAM. No, Flavia, for in such a double love I would be a traitor to you.

FL. Damiro, oh Damiro, only Irene's beauty satisfies you, and Flavia does not seem attractive to your eyes.

DAM. I'm not saying that you are not beautiful. I say only that love is a fate; it is not one's genius, it is a force of the stars. I'm not saying, etc.

Scene xii
FLAVIA

O what a cold frost is settling in my bosom, and condensing around my heart, and filling me with an unaccustomed pain.

To this new trouble my soul has given itself over entirely. Such a tyrannical torment can be nothing else than jealousy. To this, etc.

Scene xiii
IRENE *and* ILISO

IL. O most ungrateful Irene, have you been unwilling to comfort him who is in torment for you, even by a single glance?

Ir. Ti lagni a torto .
　　Sentimi ; vagheggiarti
　　In faccia d' Eraclea ,
　　Senza periglio mio come potei?
Il. Non potefti ad Ilifo,
　　Ma potefti a Damiro
　　Volgere un guardo, un rifo,
　　Tinta d'amore, e di pietade il volto.
Ir. Io? non èver .
Il. Tu, infida.
Ir. Eh che fei ftolto .
Il. Sì mi tradifti, sì
　　Menfognera crudel .
Ir. Non è così.
Il E non vvoi che gelofa
　　Si quereli di tè l' anima mia ?
Ir. (Ora intendo cofa è la gelofia)
Il. Parla in liberi accenti,
　　E non tenermi più tra il foco,e il ghiaccio,
　　Forfe più non mi vvoi,più non ti piaccio?
Ir. 　　Mi piaci sì ; ma tù
　　Se foffi men gelofo
　　Mi piarefti più.
　　Se volgo ad uno i guardi,
　　Se movo i labri a rifo
　　Torbido tu mi guardi
　　Tutto ti cangi in vifo ,
　　E dici che amorofo
　　Il guardo,e il rifo fù.
　　Mi piaci,&c.

S C E N A XIV.

Ilifo .

COn quefte luci iftefle
　　Veggo i fuoi tradimenti,e a me li nega,
　　E quel ch'è peggio ancora ,
　　　　　　　　Me-

Meno gelofo in tanti oltraggi miei
Efler degg'io per più piacere a lei .
　　Irene mi tradifce ,
　　E no'l dovria mai far .
　　Per lei fe tutta amore ,
　　Queft'anima languifce ,
　　E come hà tanto core?
　　Come mi può ingannar ?
Irene, &c.

S C E N A XV.

Eraclea, e Decio .

Er. DEcio troppo m'offendi,
　　Se vacillando intorno a la mia fede
　　Moftri che a me il tuo cor crede, e non
Dec. Arde d'amor Marcello, 　　(crede
　　Temo non già di te, temo di quello.
Er. Fugga dal cor la gelofia bandita .
Dec. Bellezza eftrema a le rapine invita.
Er. Scufami Decio il tuo fofpetto è vano,
　　Io non fon tanto bella,egli è Romano.
　　Pofs'io di te lagnarmi.
Dec. Perche?
Er. Se in quefta Reggia
　　Per me venifti, a che venir con quella
　　Non fpiacente Donzella?
Dec. Lilla Donna non è,Livio fi chiama
　　Garzonetto, che sà
　　Eflere in verde età fido, e fagace:
　　Vedi quant'era il tuo penfier fallace.
Er. Credo agl'accenti tuoi.
Dec. Or lagnati di me, cara, fe puoi.
Er. E tu Decio a me credi ?
Dec. Sì, ma vorrei....
Er. Che chiedi?
Dec. Una lieve mercè,

B 3　　　　　　Ri-

IR. You are wrong in complaining. Listen to me: how could I show you favor, with Eraclea looking on, without danger to myself?

IL. You couldn't turn your glance, your smile, with your face colored with love and pity, to Iliso, but you could to Damiro.

IR. I? That is not true.

IL. You faithless one!

IR. Oh, you are foolish.

IL. Yes, you have betrayed me, cruel, lying one.

IR. It is not so.

IL. And you don't want my jealous soul to complain of you?

IR. (Now I understand what jealousy is.)

IL. Speak freely, and don't keep me between fire and ice any longer. Perhaps you don't want me any more, don't like me any more?

IR. I like you, yes; but I would like you better if you were less jealous. If I look at anyone, if I smile, you look angrily at me. Your expression is all changed, and you say that my glance and my smile were amorous. I like you, etc.

Scene xiv
ILISO

With these very eyes I see her betrayal, and she denies it to me; and, worse yet, I am expected to be less jealous, in the midst of the outrages against me, to please her better.

Irene is betraying me, and she should never do it. If this heart is yearning, all lovingly, for her, how can she have the heart, how can she deceive me so? Irene is betraying, etc.

Scene xv
ERACLEA *and* DECIO

ER. Decio, you offend me too much if you hesitate concerning my faith and show that your heart both believes and does not believe in me.

DEC. Marcello is burning with love. I fear, not on your account, but on his.

ER. Let jealousy be banished and flee from your heart.

DEC. Extreme beauty is an invitation to violent deeds.

ER. Forgive me, Decio, your suspicion is unfounded. I am not all that beautiful, and he is a Roman. I have grounds for complaint about you.

DEC. Why?

ER. If you came to this palace on my account, why come with that not unattractive damsel?

DEC. Lilla is not a woman. His name is Livio, a boy who knows how, in his green years, to be faithful and wise. You see how erroneous your notion was.

ER. I believe what you say.

DEC. Now complain of me, beloved, if you can.

ER. And you, Decio, do you believe in me?

DEC. Yes, but I would like . . .

ER. What is it you ask?

Ricordati.....

Er. Di che?

Dec. Ricordati,ch'io t'amo,e servo,e taccio
E s'hai pietà di me ,
Non mi mancar di fè,
Ch'io vivere non bramo ad altra in
Ricordati, &c.   (braccio.

Nel partire vede Marcello che viene, e torna
ad Eraclea .

Ecco Marcello viene ,
Mio bell'Idolo amato
Freddo più del' usato
Del mio timor torno a sentire il ghiaccio,
Ricordati ch'io t'amo, e servo, e taccio.

S C E N A XVI.

Marcello, e detti.

Mar. ERaclea , da un tuo sguardo
Destar m'intesi, e mille vampe, e

Der. (Oh Dio)   (mille.

Er. Le mie pupille
Fiamme destar non sanno ,
Perche fiamme non hanno.

Mar. Come se tutto avvampo ?
Come? s'ai raggi tuoi tutto mi sfaccio ?

Dec. Ricordati ch'io t'amo,e servo,e taccio.
      piano ad Eracl.

Er. Famoso Eroe non deviar gli spirti
Dal sentiero del'armi ,
Ne confondere insieme,e lauri,e mirti .

Mar. Bella in giorno sì chiaro,
E vinto, e vincitore,
Cingo di lauri il crin, di mirti il core .

Er. Sovengati Marcello,
Che schivi degl'ardori ,
Strepitan tra le fiamme arsi gl'allori .
      Mar.

Mar. Se tu vvoi che mi giovi il tuo consiglio,
Di che non splenda tanto al tuo bel ciglio

Dec. Eraclea .

Mostra di replitare il verso Ricordati,&c.
con atti muti .

Mar. Non poss'io
Senz'ardere il cor mio,
I lampi sostener de le tue faci.

Er. Mi ricordo che m'ami,e servi,e taci .
      piano a Decio .

Mar. Principessa,deh senti

Er. Dimmi da me che vvoi?

Mar. S'ai miei voti consenti
Vuò nel tuo Regio albergo
Quando a le nostre luci il Sol s'asconde,
Trarre in veglia festiva ore gioconde .

Er. Troppo m'onori:Olà parti Aldimira ,
E nobile apparato
Per gran danza Real fa che s'appresti .

Dec. E tu sola qui resti?   *piano tra loro.*

Er. Vanne e riposa a la mia fede in braccio.

Dec. Ricordati ch'io t'amo,e servo,e taccio.

S C E N A XVII.

Marcello, ed Eraclea .

Er. TU che d'armate genti
Duce intrepido, e forte
Vai negl'aspri cimenti ,
A vilipender da vicin la morte
Del mio ciglio negletto ai primi sguardi,
Subito t'innamori, e subit'ardi?

Mar. Sì già tutto ai tuoi lumi m'avvampo,
Del tuo ciglio m'impiaga lo strale ,
Quell'amore che nasce in un lampo;
E l'amor che sì chiama fatale.
Sì già,&c.

      B 4   SCE-

DEC. A small favor. Remember . . .

ER. What?

DEC. Remember that I love you, serve you, and am silent. And if you have pity on me, do not be unfaithful to me, for I do not want to live in anyone else's arms. Remember, etc. (*On leaving*, DECIO *sees* MARCELLO *approaching and returns to* ERACLEA.) Here is Marcello approaching. My fair beloved idol, I feel the ice of my fear returning even colder than usual. Remember that I love you, serve you, and am silent.

Scene xvi
MARCELLO *and the aforementioned*

MAR. Eraclea, I have felt a thousand, and again a thousand flames arising from one glance of yours.

DEC. (Oh Heavens!)

ER. My eyes cannot kindle flames, because they have no flames.

MAR. What? If I am all afire? What? If I am wholly melted in your rays?

DEC. Remember that I love you, serve you, and am silent (*sotto voce to* ERACLEA).

ER. Renowned hero, do not deflect your mind from the path of war, mingling laurels and myrtles together.

MAR. Fair one, on such a glorious day, as both conquered and conqueror, I encircle my brow with laurels and my heart with myrtles.

ER. Remember, Marcello, that laurels are averse to heat and crackle amid the flames.

MAR. If you want my advice to be helpful to you, tell your fair brow not to be so resplendent.

DEC. Eraclea . . . (*acts out the verse "Remember, etc."* *in dumb show*).

MAR. I cannot withstand the glow of your eyes without setting my heart afire.

ER. I remember that you love me, serve me, and are silent (*sotto voce* to DECIO).

MAR. Princess, ah, hear me.

ER. Tell me, what do you want from me?

MAR. If you grant my wishes, I desire to pass joyful hours in a feast in your royal palace, when the sun hides himself from our view.

ER. You do me too much honor. Go, Aldimira, and have noble arrangements made for a great royal ball.

DEC. And are you staying here alone?

ER. Go, and be assured of my faithfulness.

DEC. Remember that I love you, serve you, and am silent.

Scene xvii
MARCELLO *and* ERACLEA

ER. You who, as the fearless leader of armed troops, go bravely into bitter combat, to contemn death at first hand—have you so suddenly fallen in love and become all aflame, from my disheveled brow, at first sight?

MAR. Yes, I am already afire for your eyes; the arrow of your brow has wounded me. That love which is born in a flash is the love which is called fated. Yes, I am already, etc.

SCENA XVIII.

Eraclea.

O Quanto forza havete ,   (core
   E nel mondo , e nel Cielo, e in ogni
Saette inevitabili d'amore.
     Ogn'un d'amor si lagna ,
      D'amor mi lagno anch'io .
     Ardon d'amor le Stelle,
     Le piante, i sassi, il fiore,
     Languiscono d'amore
     Le meste Tortorelle,
     E innamorato bagna
     Le verdi sponde il Rio.
Tutto,&c.

Fine dell' Atto Primo.

AT-

ATTO II.

SCENA PRIMA.

Sala apparata per solenne Festino.

Eraclea , Marcello , Flavia , Irene , Damiro,
Iliso , Livio , e Decio in abito d'Uomo con
altre Dame , e Cavalieri tutti con
maschere , ora in volto , ora in
mano .

Mar. Tutto rapito in questa
    Degna pompa festiva
Stupido vò girando i lumi attenti .
Er. Marcello, e qual stupore in te si desta ,
   Se là del Tebro in riva ,
   Hai gl'occhi avvezzi a rimirar portenti?
Mar Mà quì risplende il lampo
   Del'accese tue ciglia ,
   E si cangia ogni cosa in meraviglia .
Dec. (E pur d'amor raggiona.)
Er. Alto Eroe mi perdona,
   Con piacevoli modi
   Son di rossore mio queste tue lodi.
Il. Senti Irene .
Ir. Non lice ,
   Vede la Genitrice.
Dam. Peno per te .
            furtivamente trà loro .
Ir. Per te languisco.
Il. (Oh Dio)
Fl. Caro Damiro mio
   Se non amore, almen pietà conserva.
Dam. Taci, Eraclea t'offerva .

B   I.la

Scene xviii
ERACLEA

Oh how much force you have, both on earth and in heaven, and in every heart, oh unescapable arrows of love!

Everyone complains of love, and I too complain of love. The stars burn with love; the plants, the rocks, the flowers, the sad turtledoves pine for love; and the enamored river bathes the green banks with tears. Everyone, etc.

ACT II

Scene i

A banquet hall, prepared for a solemn feast; ERACLEA, MARCELLO, FLAVIA, IRENE, DAMIRO, ILISO, LIVIO, *and* DECIO *in men's clothing, with other ladies and gentlemen, all with masks, some on their faces, others in their hands.*

MAR. All amazed by this fine festive pomp, I keep looking around attentively.

ER. Marcello, what amazement is aroused in you, if there, on the banks of the Tiber, your eyes are accustomed to seeing wonders?

MAR. But here shines the flash of your blazing eyebrows, and everything is turned into a marvel.

DEC. (He's still talking of love!)

ER. Exalted hero, forgive me, but these praises and pleasing manners of yours give me cause to blush.

IL. Listen, Irene.

IR. It's not permitted, my mother is looking.

DAM. I am in torments for you.   }*(sotto voce to each*

IR. I am pining for you.   *other)*

IL. Oh Heavens!

FL. My dear Damiro, show, if not love, at least pity.

DAM. Hush, Eraclea is looking at you.

Liv. (O che intrichi d'amore)
Er. (Decio non vedo, e lo sospira il core)
Dec. (Mi tiene occulto un mio pensier geloso)
Fl. Ascolta.....
Dam. Deh non più .
Il. Fiera .
Ir. (Nojoso)
Mar. Amato Idolo bello,
    Adorata mia Dea.
Er. Rammentati Marcello,
    Che parli ad Eraclea.
Dec (Moro di gelosia)
Er. Lilla sai tù dove Aldimira sia?
Li. Serenissima nò,
    (E'presente lo sò)
Mar. Che bianca fronte, che pupilla bruna.
Il. Dimmi.....
Ir. T'accheta.
Fl. Barbaro.
Dam. (Importuna)
Mar. Guancia di rose, labra di corallo.
Er. Signor se vuoi, si dia principio al ballo .
Mar. Facciasi quanto chiedi.
Er. Vanne Marcello, e siedi.
Mar. Servir prima ti deggio.   le dà il braccio.
Er. Io nol ricuso .
Dec (l'emo d'esser deluso)   dà il braccio a
Li. Gratie a Vossignoria.   (Livio
Fl. Crudo.   a Damiro che dà il braccio ad Ir
Il. Infedele.   ad Ir. che si fà servir da Damiro.
Dam. Mio core .
        furtivamente tra loro .
Ir. Anima mia .
Si comincia a suonare un ballo , ed in queste
mentre gl'uomini accompagnano le donne
a sedere, e poi vanno loro a sederseli in
faccia, e doppo fatto uno, o più
balli, si leva in piedi Marcello,
e và per ballare con Erac.   Mar.

Mar. Bella Eraclea se no'l ricevi ad onta,
    Meco a danzar t'invito .
Er. Signor eccomi pronta.
      dà la mano a Marcello
Dec. (Io son smarrito)
Vanno Marc ed Eraclea per ballare , e sonata
    la prima parte del ballo senza moversi
       Marcello dice.
Mar. In te mi fisso, e Amore
    M'incatena le piante al par del core .
Dec. (Come attento la guarda!)
Er. Deh ritorna in te stesso.
Dec. (E ancor si tarda?)
Mar. Dunque tu vuoi ch'io mora?
Liv. (E non si balla ancora ?)
Mar. Dunque sospiro in vano?
Dec. (O danzi , o lasci ad Eraclea la mano)
Si leva in piedi Dec. con la maschera in volto
    e và dietro a Marcello, & ad Eraclea.
Er. Serba a tempo migliore
    Il parlarmi d'amore .
Mar. Ah crudele , ah tiranna,
    Forsett son molesto?
Er. Datti pace o Signor.
In questo punto Decio stacca la mano di Marc.
    da quella d' Eraclea , e Marcello leva la
      maschera dal volto a Decio , e vuol
       mettere mano alla spada, e tutti
        si levano in piedi.
Mar Che ardire è questo?
    Temerario morrai.
Dec. Raffrena l'ira.   ridente
Er. (Decio!)
Mar. Sei tù Aldimira?   si rasserena
Fl.
Ir.   a 2. Che ravviso !
Dam.
Il.   a 2. Che veggio !

          B 6   Dec.

LI. (Oh, what complications of love!)

ER. (I do not see Decio, and my heart is sighing for him!)

DEC. (A jealous thought of mine is keeping me hidden.)

FL. Listen . . .

DAM. Ah, no more!

IL. Haughty girl!

IR. (Botheracious pest!)

MAR. My fair, beloved idol, my adored goddess.

ER. Remember, Marcello, that you are speaking to Eraclea.

DEC. (I am dying of jealousy!)

ER. Lilla, do you know where Aldimira is?

LI. Your Excellency, no. (He is here, I know.)

MAR. What an ivory brow, what a dark eye!

IL. Tell me . . .

IR. Be silent!

FL. Barbarian!

DAM. (Pest!)

MAR. Cheeks of rose, lips of coral.

ER. My lord, if it is your wish, let the dance begin.

MAR. Let your wishes be fulfilled.

ER. Go, Marcello, and be seated .

MAR. I must escort you first.

ER. I do not refuse.

DEC. (I am afraid I shall be disappointed.) *(gives his arm to* LIVIO)

LI. Thank you, my lord.

FL. Cruel one! *(to* DAMIRO, *who gives his arm to* IRENE)

IL. Faithless one! *(to* IRENE, *who is escorted by* DAMIRO)

DAM. My heart! ⎫
IR. My soul! ⎬ *(furtively to each other)*

(Dance music begins while the men escort the ladies to their seats and then sit opposite them. After one or

more dances have taken place, MARCELLO *stands and goes to dance with* ERACLEA.)

MAR. Fair Eraclea, if you do not consider it beneath your dignity, I invite you to dance with me.

ER. My lord, I am ready. *(gives her hand to* MARCELLO)

DEC. (I am lost!)

*(*MARCELLO *and* ERACLEA *go to dance, and after they have remained motionless during the first part of the dance,* MARCELLO *says:)*

MAR. I look at you and Love enchains my feet as he does my heart.

DEC. (How fixedly he stares at her!)

ER. Ah, come back to yourself!

DEC. (And are they still delaying?)

MAR. So do you want me to die?

LI. (Aren't they dancing yet?)

MAR. So am I sighing in vain?

DEC. (Let him either dance or let go of Eraclea's hand!)

*(*DECIO *stands up, with his mask on his face, and goes in back of* MARCELLO *and* ERACLEA.)

ER. Keep talk of love for a better time.

MAR. Ah, cruel one, ah, tyrannical one, perhaps I am obnoxious to you?

ER. Be reassured, my lord.

(At this point DECIO *takes* MARCELLO's *hand off* ERACLEA's. MARCELLO *takes* DECIO's *mask off his face and starts to put his hand on his sword. All rise.)*

MAR. What daring is this? Rash fellow, you shall die.

DEC. Restrain your wrath *(laughing).*

ER. (Decio!)

MAR. Are you Aldimira? *(calms down)*

FL. ⎫
IR. ⎬ *(together)* What do I behold?

DAM. ⎫
IL. ⎬ *(together)* What do I see?

Dec. Signor perdon ti chieggio,
    Se il mio scherzo ti spiacque,
    Ch'esser d'oltraggio tuo non fù mia brama.
Mar. Non è d'offesa al Cavalier la Dama.
Er. O come agl'occhi miei,
    Mascharata così bella tu sei.
Mar. Non viddi mai sotto virile ammanto,
    Donna, che al Uom si rassomigli tanto.
Er. Sino a mio nuovo cenno, in queste spoglie
    Mi servirai
Dec. Secondarò tue voglie.
Liv. (Meglio andar non potea.)
Mar. Lodo sì bel pensier; viva Eraclea.
Tutti. Eraclea viva
Mar. E intanto,
    Dia termine a la veglia, e ballo, e canto.
        Erac. tien per mano Marc. e Decio
Er. Son nemici, e vanno insieme,
    E l'amore, e gelosia.
Fl.
Ir. a 2. Son nemici, &c.
Mar.
Dec. a 2 Alma amante che non teme,
    Vero amor non sà che sia.
Dam.
Il. a 2 Alma, &c.
Er.   Son nemici, &c.
Tutti. Son nemici, &c.

SCENA II.

Livio, e Alfeo.

Liv. Alfeo giungesti tardi.
Alf. Già finito è il tripudio?
Liv. Sì: mà dove sin'ora?
Alf. Son stato in studio:

Dim.

    Dimmi Lilla chi c'era?
Liv. C'era l'Uomo, la Donna,
    La cosa forastiera.
Alf. Sempre co i tuoi strambotti.
Liv. Io con gl'Uomini dotti
    Discorrer soglio in punta di forchetta.
Alf. Ah Lilletta, Lilletta.
Liv. Quanto sei caro, saporito, e gajo.
Alf. Mi viene per la vita il formicajo.
Liv. Perche ti storci tanto?
Alf. Lilla non starmi accanto.
Liv. Per qual ragion?
Alf. Parlando con modestia,
    Se vado in bestia non havrai riparo.
Liv. Che diventi tal'or lupo mannaro?
Alf. Son lupo d'amore,
        Lilluccia mia bella.
Liv. Se brami un Agnella
        Mio bene son quà.
Alf. Già s'agita il core
        Con avide brame.
Liv. Eh mangia s'hai fame
        Non stare così.
    Son lupo, &c.

SCENA III.

Marcello, e Decio.

Mar. BElla soccorri oh Dio
    Il mio povero core.
Dec. Chiedi, che far poss'io?
Mar. Puoi ritornare in vita uno che more.
    D'Eraclea sono amante,
    Ed ella par che gl'amor miei derida,
    Dille, ch'io vivo in tante pene, e tante,
    Dille che sia pietosa, o che m'uccida.
    Nulla rispondi, e stai così sospesa?
Li.   Dec.

DEC. My lord, I beg your pardon, if my jest displeased you, for it was not my desire to offend you.
MAR. The lady gives no offense to the gentleman.
ER. Oh, how handsome you seem to my eyes, disguised in this way.
MAR. I never saw a woman who, in man's garb, resembled a man so much.
ER. Until I tell you differently, you will attend me in these clothes.
DEC. I shall follow your wishes.
LI. (It couldn't go any better!)
MAR. I praise such a good idea; hurrah for Eraclea!
ALL Hurrah for Eraclea!
MAR. And meanwhile, let us end the ball with dance and song.
(ERACLEA *holds* MARCELLO *and* DECIO *by the hands.*)
ER. Love and jealousy are enemies, but go together.
FL.
IR. *(together)* Love and jealousy, etc.
MAR. *(together)* A loving soul which knows no
DEC.   fear does not know what love is.
DAM.
IL. *(together)* A loving soul, etc.
ER. Love and jealousy, etc.
ALL Love and jealousy, etc.

Scene ii
LIVIO *and* ALFEO

LI. Alfeo, you have arrived too late.
AL. Are the festivities over?

LI. Yes; but where have you been up to now?
AL. I have been in my study. Tell me, Lilla, who was there?
LI. There was the man, the woman, and the foreign thing.
AL. Always your riddles!
LI. I always speak affectedly with learned men.
AL. Ah, Lilletta, Lilletta!
LI. How loveable, interesting, and cheerful you are!
AL. I itch all around my waist.
LI. Why are you wriggling so?
AL. Lilla, don't come near me.
LI. Why not?
AL. Speaking modestly, if I become bestial, you will have no safety.
LI. Are you turning into a werewolf?
AL. I am a lovewolf, my beautiful Lilluccia.
LI. If you want a lamb, my beloved, I am here.
AL. My heart is already pounding with avid desires.
LI. Eh, eat if you're hungry; don't stand still like that.
I am a lovewolf, etc.

Scene iii
MARCELLO *and* DECIO

MAR. Fair lady, in Heaven's name, aid my poor heart.
DEC. Just ask; what can I do?
MAR. You can restore a dying man to life. I am in love with Eraclea, and she seems to be mocking my love. Tell her that I am living in endless torment. Tell her to take pity on me or to kill me. You do not answer; are you so hesitant?

Dec. Signor m'inviti a troppo dura imprefa;
　Pur farò quanto brami
　A danno mio (fi crederà che l'ami)
Mar. A tuo danno?
Dec. A mio danno.
　Darmi peggiore affanno
　La forte non potea:
　Ah Marcello, Marcello, ami Eraclea.
Mar. E quefto amor ti fpiace?
Dec. Turba al mio fen la pace,
　Toglie al'alma il ripofo,e fà ch'io chiami
　Crudo il deftin(fi crederà che l'ami)
Mar. (Quefta di mè s'accefe)
Dec. E non intendi ancor?
Mar. (Marcello intefe)
　Scopri perche ti fpiaccia,
　Ch'arda per Eraclea.
Dec. Convien ch'io taccia.
Mar. Dunque agl'affanni miei,
　Per me da lei non cercherai riftoro?
Dec. Tanto in pregio mi fei,
　Che le dirò che tempri il tuo martoro,
　Ma s'ella ti conforta,
　Al'or di pure, che Aldimira è morta.
　　　　　vuol partire.
Mar. Fermati,e fenti.
Dec. Oh Dio,
　Che vuoi più dal cor mio,
　Se quel che brami è di mia doglia eftrema
　E per gradirti il faccio?
Mar. Vuò faper la tua pena.
Dec. Io fervo, e taccio.
Mar. Mi fà pietà quel duolo,
　Che moftri in volto,e il volto tuo fcolora.
Dec. Vedi il mio duol, ma noi conofci an-
Mar. Narrami in chiari accenti, (cora
　Donde nafcono in te tanti tormenti.
Dec. Afcolta, e per mia pace,
　　　　　　　Com-

　Compatifci chi ama,e ferve,e tace.
　La mia tiranna,
　　E'gelofia,
　　Quefta veleno
　　Mi ftilla in feno,
　　Quefta m'affligge,
　　Quefta m'affanna,
　　Quefta trafigge
　　L'anima mia.
　La mia, &c.

SCENA IV.

Marcello.

O Se cangiaffe amore
　A la mia bella il core,
E daffe a lei quel,che Aldimira hà in petto,
E a quefta in fen,quel d'Eraclea chiudeffe,
Difprezzato, e negletto
Io non vedrei le mie fperanze oppreffe,
Aldimira per me non peneria,
E la bella Eraclea farebbe mia.
　Quefti cori fe amore cangiaffe,
　Che bel cambio farebbe l'amore,
　L'uno, e l'altro fe loco mutaffe,
　Mutarebbe fortuna il mio core.
Quefti, &c.

SCENA V.

Damiro, e Irene.

Ir. Già poffo ftar ficura
　Del'amor tuo?
Dam. La fede mia te'l giura.
Ir. Ma pur Flavia amerai.
Dam. Quefto non farà mai.

　　　　　Ir.

DEC. My lord, you are asking too difficult an undertaking of me. Yet I shall do what you desire, to my own disadvantage. (He will think I am in love with him.)

MAR. To your disadvantage?

DEC. To my disadvantage. Fate could not give me a harder task. Ah, Marcello, Marcello, you love Eraclea.

MAR. And does this love displease you?

DEC. It disturbs the peace of my bosom. It takes away the calm of my soul and makes me call destiny cruel. (He will think I am in love with him.)

MAR. (She has fallen in love with me.)

DEC. And do you still not understand?

MAR. (Marcello has understood.) Tell me why you do not like me to be in love with Eraclea.

DEC. I must remain silent.

MAR. So you will not seek from her, on my behalf, relief from my torments?

DEC. I esteem you so much that I shall tell her to relieve your pain; but if she gives you comfort, then say too that Aldimira is dead. (starts to leave)

MAR. Stay and listen.

DEC. Oh Heavens, what more do you want from my heart, if what you want causes me extreme sorrow and I do it to please you?

MAR. I want to know what is your sorrow.

DEC. I serve, and am silent.

MAR. This unhappiness, which you show in your countenance and which draws the color from your features, excites my pity.

DEC. You see my unhappiness, but you do not yet know what it is.

MAR. Tell me in plain words, what is the source of such great torment for you.

DEC. Listen, and, for my peace of mind, have sympathy with one who loves, serves, and is silent. My tyrant is jealousy. She distills poison in my bosom; she afflicts me and troubles me; she pierces my soul. My tyrant, etc.

Scene iv
MARCELLO

Oh, if Love were to change my lady's heart and were to give her the one that Aldimira has in her bosom and give Aldimira the one that Eraclea has, I would not be despised and rejected and would not see my hopes dashed. Aldimira would not be tormented on my account, and the fair Eraclea would be mine.

If love were to exchange these hearts, what a fine exchange Love would make. If the two were to change places, my heart would change fortune. If love, etc.

Scene v
DAMIRO *and* IRENE

IR. Can I be assured of your love?

DAM. My faith swears it to you.

IR. But yet you will love Flavia.

DAM. This will never be.

Ir. Ah fe l'amaffi tu, mi fpiaceria,
    Ch'io conofco cos'è la gelofia.
Dam. Deh non temer mio bene,
    Non pavèntar mio fole.
Ir. Cosi dolci parole
    M'hanno un foco foave in petto accefo,
    Che mai più non l'hò intefo.
Dam. Ora il tuo core a ben amare impara,
    (Quanto è femplice più, tanto è più cara)
Ir. Prima ftandoti appreffo,
    Io godea di mirarti,
    Come ancor godo di mirarti ad effo,
    Ma fol negl'occhi al'or mi ftava amore,
    Or fento, che pafsò dagl'occhi al core.
Dam. Irene mia, già che per me t'accendi,
    Ad effer fida apprendi,
    E fe da grave duolo,
    Non vuoi ch'io refti ucciſo, amami folo.
Ir. Damiro, an'ma mia,
    Che tu ancor fai cos'è la gelofia?
Dam. Sono amante gelofo
    De le bellezze tue.
Ir. Datti ripofo:
    Irene farà fida,
    Che non defio, che grave duol t'uccida.
Dam.   Io t'amo, ma fola,
    E folo, ben mio,
    Vogl'effere anch'io
    Amato da te.
    Queft'alma confola,
    Che lieto un amante,
    Non gode un iftante,
    Se folo non è.
    Io t'amo, &c.

SCE

Irene, Iliſo.

Il. (Ecco la mia ribella)
Ir.   Perchè turbato ftai?
Il. Ingrata ben lo fai (fempre è più bella)
Ir. Qualche nuovo delirio
    Agita il tuo penfiéro?
Il. Ama Damiro.
Ir. Puoi dir ch'io ti tradifco?
Il. E tu me'l puoi negar?
Ir. Ti compatifco.
Il. Effer così derifo
    Più non voglio da te.
Ir. Povero Iliſo.
Il. Con fentimenti infidi
    Ofcurando ti vai.
Ir. Troppo mi fgridi.
Il. Ti fgrido sì, perche infedel tu fei,
    Godi de torti miei,
    Ridi del mio cordoglio....
Ir. Come?
Il. Perfida và.
Ir. Non tanto orgoglio.
Il. Io fon quel, che ti piacqui, ed io fon quello
    A cui giuravi ogn'ora
    Di non mancar già mai,
    Io fon quel che t'amai,
    E quel, che t'amo, a mio difpetto ancora,
    E tu congiando amore,
    Vai teffendo al tuo core
    Altra rete, altro laccio,
    Forfe più non mi vuoi, più non ti piaccio?
Ir.   Più non ti voglio nò, più non mi piaci,
    Se un tempo eri il mio bello,
    Ed or non fei più quello,

Dim-

IR. Oh, if you loved her, I would dislike it, for I know what jealousy is.

DAM. Nay, do not fear, my love, do not be afraid, my sun.

IR. These words so sweet have kindled a gentle blaze in my heart, such as I never felt before.

DAM. Now your heart is learning how to love well. (The simpler she is, the dearer she is.)

IR. Formerly, when I was near you, I enjoyed looking at you, as I still do enjoy gazing on you. But then Love was only in my eyes; now I feel he has passed from my eyes into my heart.

DAM. My Irene, now that you are in love with me, learn to be faithful, and if you don't want me to be killed by intense sorrow, love me alone.

IR. Damiro, my soul, do you know yet what jealousy is?

DAM. I am a lover, jealous of your beauty.

IR. Be reassured; Irene will be faithful, for I do not desire to have intense sorrow kill you.

DAM. I love you, but you alone; and, my beloved, I too want to be loved by you. Comfort this heart, for a lover does not enjoy a single minute, if he is not the only one. I love you, etc.

Scene vi
IRENE *and* ILISO

IL. (Here is my faithless one!)
IR. Why are you upset?

IL. Ungrateful one, you know full well. (She is ever more beautiful!)

IR. Is some madness disturbing your thoughts?

IL. You love Damiro.

IR. Can you say I am betraying you?

IL. Can you deny it?

IR. I'm sorry for you.

IL. I won't be mocked this way by you any longer.

IR. Poor Iliso!

IL. You are darkening your soul with faithless sentiments.

IR. You are scolding me too much.

IL. Yes, I am scolding you, because you are faithless. You enjoy the wrong you do me, you laugh at my grief . . .

IR. What?

IL. Unfaithful girl, get along with you!

IR. Don't be so stuck up!

IL. I am the one you loved, and I am the one to whom you were continually swearing you would be true. I am the one who loved you, and who, to my regret, still love you, whereas you, changing your love, are weaving for your heart another net, another snare. Perhaps you don't want me any more, you don't like me any more?

IR. I don't want you any more, no, I don't like you any more. If, once upon a time, you were my be-

Dimmi,che far fi può?foffrilo,e taci
Piu, &c.

SCENA VII.

Iliso,e Flavia.

Il. PEr mio maggior martire
  Aggiungi anima rea gli fcherni al'òte?
Fl. (Tutto nubi la fronte
  Sparge le ciglia fue di fdegni,e d'ire)
  E qual cagione a fufcitar ti viene
  'Tanto furor?
Il. L'infedeltà d'Irene :
  Son tradito da lei.
Fl. Dunque avvifto ti fei,
  Ch'ella Damiro adora.
Il. Per lui mi fdegna, e mi fchernifce acora;
  Si dà core più infido,
  Più crudel, più fallace.
Fl. Ilifo datti pace.
Il. E troppo grave il torto.
Fl. Ambo,fe vuoi,potremo haver conforto.
  Da Irene tua tu difprezzato fei,
  E da Damiro mio fprezzata io fui,
  S'ella non t'ama,io t'amerò per lei,
  E s'ei non m'ama, amami tù per lui.
Il. Sì, rifolvo d'amarti,
  Pur che fe mi prometta:
  Farà de noftri oltraggi amor vendetta.
Fl. Sarò fedele,e forte,
  Ingannato Damiro
  Da la fua falfa fpene,
  Reftarà fenza Flavia,e fenza Irene.
Il. Ed io vedrò l'ingrata,
  Che tanto m'hà derifo,
  Reftar fenza Damiro,e fenza Ilifo. *parte.*
    Fl.

Fl. Chi lafcia la fua bella,
  E un altra amar ne vuole,
  Perdendo, e quefta, e quella
  Refta delufo un dì.
  A un incoftante Amante,
  Sò che più volte fuole
  Succedere così.
Chi,&c.

SCENA VIII.

Delitiofa con cafcate d'acqua.

Eraclea , poi Marcello, e Decio.

Er. COntentatevi almeno
  Miei penfieri amorofi,
  Ch'io prenda nel dormir brevi ripofi
    Si mette a federe per dormire,poi uice.
  Ma che brami Eraclea,che fai, che tenti?
  Sai pur tu che gl'amanti
  Han lumi da mirare i lor tormenti,
  Han luci avvezze a partorir più ftille,
  Ma fol per ripofar non han pupille.
  Veglino gl'occhi, e fegua
  A contemplare i fuoi martiri; il core:
  Val più di mille gioje un mio dolore.
    Si ferma in atto penfofo.
Mar. Parlafti ad Eraclea.
Dec. Non le parlai.
Mar. Perche?
Dec. Non ebbi mai
  Opportuno un iftante.
Er. (Che tormento foave effere amante!)
Mar. Ma là tra i fiori affifa
  Giace la vita mia; tu vanne a lei,
  Narrale i pianti miei, le mie querele.
Er. (Che bel vanto d'un alma effer fedele!)
    Dec.

---

loved, you are no longer. Tell me, what can be done about it? Suffer, and be silent. I don't want you, etc.

Scene vii
ILISO *and* FLAVIA

IL. To make me suffer more, ungrateful soul, are you adding insult to injury?
FL. (With his brow like a thundercloud, his eyes flash disdain and wrath.) What cause is arousing your anger so?
IL. Irene's faithlessness. I am betrayed by her.
FL. Then be aware that she loves Damiro.
IL. She neglects me for him, and in addition disdains me. Is there a more faithless, more cruel, more deceitful heart?
FL. Iliso, calm down.
IL. My wrongs are too great.
FL. Both of us, if you wish it, can be comforted. You are despised by your Irene, and I have been rejected by my Damiro. If she does not love you, I will love you in her stead; and if he does not love me, you love me in his stead.
IL. Yes, I will resolve to love you, provided you plight your faith to me. Love will avenge our wrongs.
FL. I will be faithful, and perhaps Damiro, deceived by his false hopes, will be left without Flavia and without Irene.
IL. And I will see the ungrateful girl, who has mocked me so, remain without Damiro and without Iliso. (*Exit.*)

FL. He who deserts his beloved and wants to make love to another will lose both, and one day will be disappointed. To an inconstant lover, I know that it often happens this way. He who, etc.

Scene viii
Wooded scene with waterfalls; ERACLEA, *and later* MARCELLO *and* DECIO.

ER. At least be content, O my thoughts of love, to let me take a brief rest in sleeping. (*Sits down to sleep, then says:*) But what are you yearning for, Eraclea, what are you doing, what are you trying to do? You, too, know that lovers have orbs to look on their torments; they have eyes accustomed to shed many tears; but only to rest, they have no eyes. Let the eyes remain awake, and let the heart continue contemplating its tortures; one of my sorrows is worth a thousand joys. (*She remains fixed in a thoughtful pose.*)
MAR. Did you speak to Eraclea?
DEC. I have not spoken to her.
MAR. Why?
DEC. I have not had a suitable moment.
ER. (What sweet torment it is to be a lover?)
MAR. But there, seated amongst the flowers, my life is seated; go to her, tell her of my weeping, my affliction.
ER. (What a beautiful boast of a soul it is, to be faithful!)

Dec. Deh vieni à la tua bella
   Tu con eſſa favella,
   Ch'io de'martiri tuoi farolle fede,
   E chiederò (mà non per te) mercede.
Mar. Mi piace il tuo conſiglio
   Andianne innanti à la real ſembianza.
Er. (Che dolce nutrimento è la ſperanza.)
Mar. Principeſſa.
Er. Marcello.
Mar. In pochi accenti
   Io torno à rinovare i miei tormenti.
Er. Taci, che cerchi oh Dio
   Eſſer empio al tuo core, e crudo al mio.
Mar. Aldimira m'aita.
Dec. Se Marcello t'invita
   A ſentire il ſuo duolo
   Tù di ſentirlo non recarti à ſdegno.
Er. Decio così raggiona?   *piano à Decio.*
Dec. E un finto impegno.   *piano ad Erac.*
Mar. T'amo ne v'à momento
   Che non habbia compagno un mio ſoſpiro
   In me, più me non ſento,
   Mà ſento amore, e l'aſpro mio martiro.
Er. Con racconti sì meſti
   Affliggi l'alma tua, la mia funeſti.
Dec. Egli del ſuo gran foco
   Par che molto habbia detto, e hà detto poco.
   Oſſerva gl'occhi ſuoi,
   E conſidera poi
   Qual ſia del cor la fiāma, il dardo, e il laccio,
   Mà rifletti, ch'io t'amo, e ſervo, e taccio.
         piano ad Erac.
   Vedi à tuo prò quanto à parlar m'accingo
         à Marc.
Marc. Ti deggio molto.
Dec. Già tu ſai ch'io fingo.   *ad Erac. piano.*
Marc. Eraclea che riſolvi?
   Ami Aldimira è verò?

                  Er.

Er. L'amo al par di me ſteſſa.
Marc. Sia la pietà ch'io ſpero
   In virtù de'ſuoi me conceſſa:
   Deh placati una volta,
   Dimmi, che penſi far?
Er. Marcello aſcolta.
   Penſo far ciò, che brami,
   S'ella dirà, ch'io t'ami,
   E che ti dia mercè;
   Mà ſe non vuol coſtei,
   Ch'Idolo mio ti chiami
   Lagnati ſol di lei
   Non ti lagnar di me.
   Penſo, &c.

S C E N A   IX.

Marcello, e Decio.

Marc. UDiſti? in tuo potere   (mia,
   Stà la mia morte, e ſtà la vita,
   Ogn'altra cura oblia,
   E pietoſa conſola i dolor miei.
Dec. Troppo ingiuſta farei.
Marc. Aldimira, che ſparſe
   A impetrarmi mercè tante preghiere,
   Mercè mi niega? ed ora,
   Che ſoccorrer mi può, non mi ſoccorre?
Dec. Marcello, altro è il pregare, altro è il diſ-
Marc. T'intendo sì, t'intendo,   (porre.
   Adorando Eraclea, ſò che t'offendo.
Dec. M'offendi è ver, mà la raggion non ſai.
Marc. Ardi per me d'amore.
Dec. Non hebbi mai sì temerario il core.
Marc. Dunque?
Dec. S'io ti ſvelaſſi
   Un alto arcano, che racchiudo in petto,
   Gl'affanni miei compatireſti al'ora,
                 Che

DEC. Ah, go yourself to your fair lady with these words, for I shall be a witness to her of your sufferings and shall ask (but not for you) mercy.

MAR. I like your advice; let us go into the royal presence.

ER. (What sweet food is hope!)

MAR. Princess!

ER. Marcello!

MAR. In a few words, I renew again my sufferings.

ER. Be silent, for, oh Heavens, you are seeking to be impious towards your own heart and cruel to mine.

MAR. Aldimira, help me.

DEC. If Marcello begs you to hear his complaint, you should not disdain to listen to him.

ER. Is this Decio speaking thus? (*sotto voce* to DECIO).

DEC. I am pretending to act on his behalf (*sotto voce to* ERACLEA).

MAR. I love you, and there is not a moment in which I do not have a sigh as my companion. I do not feel myself any longer, but I feel only love and my intense suffering.

ER. With such a sad story, you are afflicting your soul and harming mine.

DEC. He seems to have said a great deal about his great fire, and he has said only a little. Look at his eyes and then consider what the flame, the dart, and the snare of his heart must be. But remember that I love you, serve you, and am silent (*sotto voce to* ERACLEA). You see how ready I am to speak on your behalf (*to* MARCELLO).

MAR. I am greatly in your debt.

DEC. You know already that I am pretending (*sotto voce to* ERACLEA).

MAR. Eraclea, what have you decided? You love Aldimira, do you not?

ER. I love Aldimira like myself.

MAR. Let the pity which I hope for, through the merit of her pleas, be granted me. Ah, be merciful just once; tell me, what do you plan to do?

ER. Marcello, listen.
I plan to do what you desire, if she says that I should love you and show you mercy. But if she does not wish you to be called my idol, complain only of her, do not complain of me. I plan, etc.

Scene ix
MARCELLO *and* DECIO

MAR. Did you hear? My death and my life are in your hands. Forget every other care, have pity, and console my sorrows.

DEC. I would be too unfair.

MAR. Does Aldimira, who expended so many prayers to obtain mercy for me, deny me mercy? And, now that she can succor me, does not do so?

DEC. Nevertheless, it is one thing to beg, another to be in a position to decide.

MAR. I understand you, yes, I understand you. When I adore Eraclea, I know that I offend you.

DEC. You offend me, it is true, but you do not know the reason why.

MAR. You are in love with me.

DEC. My heart was never that bold.

MAR. Well, then?

DEC. If I were to reveal to you a deep secret which I keep locked in my bosom, you would sympathize

Che amore è il mio, mà nõ l' intõdi ancora.
Marc. Bella tu mi confondi,
  Il fegreto che afcondi
  Per pietà mi rivela.
Dec. Con troppa gelofia l'alma lo cela.
Marc. Di tacer ti prometto,
  E fe ad altri il confido
  Scocchi il Ciel contro me faette accefe.
Dec. Tempo verrà, che te'l farò palefe.
    Saper tu vuoi
      Quel ch'hò nel core,
      Mà fò che poi
      Ti fpiacerà;
      Non ti vedrai
      Solo in amore
      Mà troverai
      Rivalità.
  Scoprir, &c.

SCENA X.

Marcello.

O' di funefto duolo
  Infelice novella!
Mà invan bramo effer folo
In amar Eraclea, ch'è troppo bella:
L'amino pure e cento cori, e cento,
E vada il mio di fua pietade altero
Quanto farei contento; ah non lo fpero.
  Un Idolo di faffo,
    E l'Idolo che adoro:
    Di doglia in doglia io paffo
    Nè trovo mai riftoro.
  Un Idolo, &c.

SCE-

SCENA XI.

Alfeo, e poi Lilla.

Alf. PRecipitata
    Filofofia.
    E dove, e dove è andata
    La continenza mia?
    Precipitata, &c.
Lil. Lilla à te s'avvicina.
Alf. Ecco la mia ruina;
  Non me ne fò dar pace.
Lil. Dimmi forfe ti fpiace,
  Che agl'amorofi fguardi
  Rifoluto ti fei d'arder sì tardi?
Alf. Son ftato faldo tanti luftri, e poi
  Vifta la faccia tua brunetta, e bella
  Non fcefi nò, precipitai di fella.
Lil. Or che tu fei caduto
  Farai mai più con Flavia, e con Irene
  Il Satrapo d'Atene?
Alf. E fempre ben, dar buon côfiglio agl'altri.
Lil. Fan molti Vecchi fcaltri
  I corretori de la gioventù,
  Son tutti vitio, e fingono virtù.
  Strano ancora è il vedere
  Certe Donne attempate
  Far da vaghe, da belle,
  Da morte innamorate, e da Donzelle,
  E fe poi fà l'amor qualche ragazza
  Le dan nome di pazza
  Tutte fi fcandalizzano,
  E tante ciarle infilzano,
  Ch'è cofa da ftordire;
  E loro? e loro poi . . . . nol voglio dire.
Alf. Quefto è un cafo, che fpeffo
  Succederà, fuccede, ed è fucceffo;

Io

---

with my troubles, for Love is what troubles me, but you do not yet understand it.

MAR. Fair lady, you confuse me; for pity's sake, reveal to me the secret you are hiding.

DEC. My heart conceals it with too much jealousy.

MAR. I promise you to be silent, and if I disclose it to anyone else, may Heaven shoot its fiery arrows against me.

DEC. The time will come, when I will reveal it to you. You wish to know what I have in my heart, but I know that then you will not like it. You will not be alone in love, but you will find rivalry. You wish to know, etc.

Scene x
MARCELLO

Ah, what unhappy news of disastrous sorrow! But in vain I yearn to be alone in loving Eraclea, who is too fair. Let a hundred, and yet another hundred hearts love her—if mine were to be proud of enjoying her favor, how happy I would be! Ah, I do not hope for this.

An idol of stone is the idol I adore. I pass from one sorrow to another, nor do I ever find comfort. An idol of stone, etc.

Scene xi
ALFEO, *and later* LILLA

AL. Philosophy has deserted me. And where, oh where, has my self-restraint gone? Philosophy has deserted me, etc.

LI. Lilla is approaching you.

AL. Here is my ruin. I cannot find rest with regard to her.

LI. Tell me: perhaps are you displeased that you have resolved to burn with amorous glances so late in life?

AL. I have stood firm for so many decades, and then, when I saw your beautiful brunette face, I did not dismount, I fell out of the saddle.

LI. Now that you have fallen, will you still play the tyrant of Athens with Flavia and Irene?

AL. It is always well to give good advice to others.

LI. Many clever old men act like mentors of youth. They are all vice, and they pretend to virtue. It is even stranger to see certain elderly ladies act like attractive, beautiful girls, like women madly in love, and like damsels; and then, if some girl makes love, they call her foolish. They are all scandalized and string together so much gossip, that it makes you dizzy. And they? And they, then . . . I don't want to say.

AL. This is a case which often will happen, happens,

Io però ch'hò cervello
M'attacco al bono, al giovanetto, e al bello.
Lil. Io sò che non son cosa
Nè vaga, nè vezzosa,
Però son fanciulletta, e tenerella
Non hò gran polpa addosso,
Non son nemen tutt'osso,
Mà son così così rosicarella.
Io sò, &c.
Alf. Lilla mia, Lilla taci,
Tutta à genio mi vai, tutta mi piaci,
Tu per i denti miei cara mia gioja
Sei giusto un biscottino di Savoja.
Lil. Tu per farmi satolla
Un gran Pasticcio sei di pasta frolla.
Alf. Quel volto morettino,
O potenza del Mondo è pur divino,
Mi pare un Ciel di chiaro oscuro adorno
Tal quale stà sù lo spuntar del giorno.
Lil. Al manto à la figura,
A la grave struttura
A quel ventre di Bacco
Mi rassembri l'Idea del'Almanacco.
Alf. Io di tutto m'intendo
Posso de contingentibus futuris
Dar certissime nove,
E sò quando è bon tempo, e quando piove.
Lil. Io Sono ferita.
Alf. Languisco d'amore.
Lil. Sì vita.
Alf. Sì core
à 2. Mà solo per te.
Alf. (E'massimo.) *Lil.* (E'troppo.)
Alf. (Il gusto.) *Lil.* (Lo spasso.)
Mio dolce siroppo.
Alf. Già moro. *Lil.* Già passo.
Alf. Soccorso. *Lil.* Mercè.
Io sono, &c.

SCE-

SECONDO.
SCENA XII.

Flavia, e Irene.

Fla. TV di Damiro amante?
Ir. E tu d'Iliso?
Fla. Bella finezza Irene
Amare un che mi sprezza.
Ir. Flavia bella finezza
Un che stà in odio mio, chiamar tuo bene.
Fl. Forza è d'amor, che sù quest'alma impera.
Ir. Forza è di genio, che al mio cor sovrasta.
Fl. Ah Irene Irene.
Ir. Ah Flavia Flavia
à 2. Basta.
Fla. Tu che vuoi?
Ir. Tu che brami?
Fla. Nulla da te desio.
Ir. Nulla pretendo.
Fla. Ti capisco.
Ir. T'intendo.
Fla. Un maligno veleno
Ir. Un acceso furore
Fla. Contamina il tuo seno.
Ir. Arde il tuo core.
Fla. Misera.
Ir. Sventurata.
Fla. Lo veggo.
Ir. Lo discerno.
Fla. E'ferita.
Ir. E'piagata.
Fla. (Che invidioso scherno.)
Ir. (Che livido sorriso.)
Fla. Tu di Damiro amante?
Ir. E tu d'Iliso?
Giusto è il mio sdegno.
Vuol partir Irene, e s'incontra con Iliso.
C   Fl.

Scene xii

FLAVIA *and* IRENE

and has happened. But I, who have brains, attach myself to what is good, young, and beautiful.

LI. I know that I am not something which is either fair or attractive, but I am a maiden, and tender. I have not a great deal of flesh on me, nor am I all skin and bones, but I am just a tempting tidbit. I know, etc.

AL. My Lilla, my Lilla, you suit my taste exactly, you are wholly pleasing to me. You, my beloved jewel, are just a Savoy biscuit to my taste.

LI. You, to satisfy me, are a big pie of puff pastry.

AL. That dark little face, oh Powers of the Universe, is divine. It seems to me a heaven adorned with light and shade, just like the sun at daybreak.

LI. By the cloak on your figure, by your heavy build, by your Bacchus-like belly, you seem to me the ideal of the Almanac.

AL. I understand everything; I can give absolutely certain information about future events, and I know when it is good weather and when it rains.

LI. I am stricken.

AL. I am pining with love.

LI. Yes, my love . . .
AL. Yes, my heart . . . } (together) but only for you.

AL. The pleasure . . .   LI. The joke . . .
AL. . . . is extreme.   . . . is tremendous.
My sweet syrup.

AL. I am already dying.   LI. I am already passing.
AL. Help!   LI. Mercy!

I am stricken, etc.

FL. You, lover of Damiro?

IR. And you, of Iliso?

FL. This is fine courtly behavior, Irene, to love one who despises me.

IR. Flavia, it is fine courtly behavior to call one who hates me, your beloved.

FL. It is the force of love which rules over this soul.

IR. It is the force of the spirit which rules over my heart.

FL. Ah, Irene, Irene!
IR. Ah, Flavia, Flavia! } (together) Enough!

FL. What do you want?

IR. What do you wish?

FL. I desire nothing from you.

IR. I lay claim to nothing.

FL. I understand you.

IR. I comprehend you.

FL. A malign poison . . .

IR. An evil blazing fury . . .

FL. . . . defiles your bosom.

IR. . . . is setting your heart on fire.

FL. Wretch!

IR. Unfortunate!

FL. I see it.

IR. I perceive it.

FL. She is hurt.

IR. She is wounded.

FL. (What envious scorn!)

IR. (What a livid smile!)

FL. You, lover of Damiro?

IR. And you, of Iliso? My contempt is well deserved.

(IRENE *starts to exit and meets* ILISO.)

Fl. Io con ragion m'adiro .

Vuol partire Flavia, e s'incontra con Damiro .

Ir. Flavia.

Fl. Irene .

Ir. Ecco Ilifo .

Fl. Ecco Damiro .

SCENA XIII.

Ilifo, e Damiro, e dette.

Il. Alma infedele.   *piano ad Irene .*

Fl. Ingrato .   *piano a Damiro .*

Ir. Vuol così il fato.   *ad Ilifo.*

Dam. E così vuole amore.   *a Flavia.*

Il. Vanne al'Idolo tuo.   *ad Irene.*

Fl. Vanne al tuo core .   *a Damiro.*

Il. Damiro tuo deh mira ,   *ad Irene.*
   Come per te fofpira .

Fl. E tu deh guarda Irene,   *a Damiro.*
   Come per te ftà in pene.

Ir. Scorgi di Flavia in volto,   *ad Ilifo.*
   Qual duolo hà in petto accolto.

Dam. Vedi il tuo vago Ilifo   *a Flavia.*
   Sparfo d'affanni il vifo,
   Ei per te langue .

Ir. Ella per te fi muore.

Dam. Vanne al'Idolo tuo.   *a Flavia .*

Ir. Vanne al tuo core.   *ad Ilifo.*

Il. Io di Flavia mi vanto.

Dam. Son d'Irene il confeffo .

Ir. Sdegno di ftarti accanto .

Fla. Più non ti voglio appreffo .

Dam. Vieni ben mio .

Il. Vieni mio dolce amore .

Ir. Vanne al'Idolo tuo .   *a Fla.*

Fla. Vanne al tuo core.   *a Irene.*

Vanno , Irene a prender per mano Damiro , e
   Flavia a prender per mano Ilifo.

             Ir.

Ir. Damiro mi piace.

Fla. Ilifo è il mio fole.

Ir. Ti fpiace?

Fla. Ti duole ?

   a 2 Ne fento pietà.

Ir. Ma

Fla. Ma

Ir. Se chiedi. *Fla.* Se brami.

Ir. Che lafci Damiro .

Fla. Che Ilifo non ami .

Ir. E folle deliro .

Fla. E'gran vanità .

   Damiro, &c.

SCENA XIV.

Damiro, Ilifo, e poi Marcello.

Dam. Non fegui Flavia?

Il. NE tu non fegui Irene ?

Dam. Chieder ciò tu non dei .

Il. Ne a te da penfier miei cercar conviene.

Dam. Tanto ardir.

Il. Tanto orgoglio.

Dam. Soffrir non poffo,

Il. E tolerar non voglio .

Dam. Stringi la fpada.

Il. E tu l'acciaro impugna.

Dam. Al cimento. *Il.* A la pugna.
       Si vogliono battere.

Mar. Olà fermate ,
   Qual infano furore
   A duello vi chiama?

Dam. E fdegno .

Il. E amore.

Mar. E la beltà di cui voi fiete accefi ?

Dam. E di fangue Reale .

Mar. (Oh D o che intefi,

      C 2   Forfe

FL. I am justified in getting angry. (FLAVIA *starts to exit and meets* DAMIRO.)

IR. Flavia!

FL. Irene!

IR. Here is Iliso.

FL. Here is Damiro.

Scene xiii
ILISO, DAMIRO, *and the aforementioned*

IL. Faithless soul! (*sotto voce to* IRENE)

FL. Ungrateful wretch! (*sotto voce to* DAMIRO)

IR. It is Fate's decree (*to* ILISO).

DAM. And it is Love's decree (*to* FLAVIA).

IL. Go to your idol (*to* IRENE).

FL. Go to your heart (*to* DAMIRO).

IL. Ah, see how your Damiro is sighing for you (*to* IRENE).

IR. See in Flavia's face what sorrow she harbors in her bosom (*to* ILISO).

DAM. See how your charming Iliso, with his face distorted by sorrow, is pining for you.

IR. She is dying for you.

DAM. Go to your idol (*to* FLAVIA).

IR. Go to your heart (*to* ILISO).

IL. I glory in being Flavia's.

DAM. I belong to Irene, I confess it.

IR. I disdain to stand next to you.

FL. I don't want you near me any more.

DAM. Come, my beloved.

IL. Come, my sweet love.

IR. Go to your idol (*to* FLAVIA).

FL. Go to your heart (*to* IRENE).

(IRENE *goes and takes* DAMIRO *by the hand, and* FLAVIA *takes* ILISO *by the hand.*)

IR. Damiro pleases me.

FL. Iliso is my sun.

IR. Do you mind?   ⎱
FL. Does it hurt you? ⎰ (*together*) I'm sorry for it.

IR. But . . .

FL. But . . .

IR. . . . if you ask . . .

FL. . . . if you desire . . .

IR. . . . me to leave Damiro . . .

FL. . . . me not to love Iliso . . .

IR. . . . it is mad delirium.

FL. . . . it is a vain hope.
   Damiro, etc.

Scene xiv
DAMIRO, ILISO, *and later* MARCELLO

DAM. Aren't you following Flavia?

IL. And aren't you following Irene?

DAM. You have no right to ask that.

IL. And it is none of your business to inquire into my thoughts.

DAM. Such daring . . .

IL. Such haughtiness . . .

DAM. . . . I cannot endure.

IL. . . . I will not stand for.

DAM. Take your sword.

IL. And you, grasp your steel in your hand.

DAM. To the test!

IL. Have at you!

(*They start to fight.*)

MAR. Ho, there, stop! What insane madness incites you to duel?

DAM. It is disdain.

IL. It is love.

MAR. And the beauty with whom you are in love?

DAM. She is of royal blood.

MAR. (Oh, Heavens, what have I heard? Perhaps

Forfe e Damiro,e Ilifo à mio rivale)
Ceffi l'incauta lite
  Troppo amore v'acciece, e troppo ardite.
Dam. Quando è d'amor l'errore
  Colpa l'error non hà.
Il. E fe pur colpa è amore
  Merita haver pietà.
a 2. Quando, &c.

SCENA XV.

Marcello, e Decio.

Mar. GIungi a tempo Aldimira,
  Se non erra il penfiero,
  Sò perche fparga i voti al'aura errante:
  Eraclea d'altri è amante, è vero?
Dec. E vero.
Mar. Cagion de fuoi tanto fecreti affanni
  Sono, o Ilifo, o Damiro è vero?
Dec. T'inganni.
Mar. Come?
Dec. Tace non viene,
  Uno Flavia fofpira, e l'altro Irene.
Mar. Dunque?
Dec. Di te mi fido?
Mar. Saprò ferbar l'areano tuo nafcofto.
Dec. Con amor corrifpofto
  Straniero Eroe d'illuftre fangue antico,
  Ama Eraclea e d'Aldimira è amico.
Mar. Il nome?
Dec. Dir no'l poffo.
Mar. E in Siracufa?
Dec. In Siracufa.
Mar. E tanto,
  Perche adoro Eraclea
  Sei gelofa per lui,
  E ti pefan così gl'amori altrui?   (preffa,
Dec. Il Cielo in noi tanta amiftade ha im-
  Ch'io

Ch'io fento i cafi fuoi tutti in me fteffa,
  Pure a far che tu veda
  Quanto del tuo dolor cura mi prendo,
  'Tentarò lui che la fua Dea ti ceda.
Mar. Gratie o bella ti rendo;
  Affifta amore ai tuoi penfieri audaci.
Dec. Marcello ecco Eraclea, fimula, e taci.

SCENA XVI.

Eraclea, e detti.

Mar. PRincipeffa mi trovi
  Qual mi lafciafti, e l'alma,
  D'Aldimira al'arbitrio in van ricorre,
  Ch'ella del tuo defio non vuol difporre.
  Dunque bel Idol mio,
  Che rifolvi? che fai?
Er. Marcello Addio.
Mar. Crudel perche m'afcondi
  L'interno del tuo cor?
Er. Per me rifpondi.
  A Decio, e lo fà paffare in mezzo.
Mar. A tanti affanni miei
  Non havrò mai pietà?
Dec. Chiedilo a lei.
  piano a Marcello e lo fà paffare in mezzo.
Mar. Queft'alma che fofpira,
  Quando pace otterrà?
Er. Sallo Aldimira.
Mar. Care labra vivaci
  Dite ch'io mora almen.
Dec. Simula, e taci.   *piano a Marcello.*
Mar. Legiadra bocca bella,
  Dimmi un sì dimmi un nò.
Er. Parla con quella.
Mar. Non vuò pietà da lei,
  Voglio pietà da tè.

C 3   Se

Damiro and Iliso are my rivals.) Let this heedless struggle cease. You are blinded by excessive love, and you are overbold.

DAM. When the fault is one of love, the fault is not to blame.

IL. And if love is indeed a fault, it deserves to be pitied. (*together*) When, etc.

Scene xv
MARCELLO *and* DECIO

MAR. You are just in time, Aldimira. If I am not mistaken, I know why I waste my wishes on the wandering air. Eraclea is in love with another, is she not?

DEC. It is true.

MAR. The cause of her secret longing is either Iliso or Damiro, is it not?

DEC. You are wrong.

MAR. What?

DEC. You must be silent. One of them is sighing for Flavia, the other for Irene.

MAR. Well, then?

DEC. Can I trust you?

MAR. I can keep your secret hidden.

DEC. With a requited love, a foreign hero of noble descent loves Eraclea, and is a friend of Aldimira.

MAR. His name?

DEC. I cannot tell it.

MAR. Is he in Syracuse?

DEC. In Syracuse.

MAR. And, because I worship Eraclea, are you so jealous on his account, and are others' loves of such concern to you?

DEC. Heaven has imposed such friendship on us, that I feel all his concerns as my own. And yet, to prove to you how much I take your sorrow to heart, I shall try to persuade him to yield his goddess to you.

MAR. I give you thanks, O fair lady; may Love help your daring plans.

DEC. Marcello, here is Eraclea; pretend, and be silent.

Scene xvi
ERACLEA *and the aforementioned*

MAR. Princess, you find me and my heart just as you left me. It has recourse to Aldimira in vain, for she is not willing to command your desire. So then, fair idol of mine, what have you decided? What will you do?

ER. Marcello, farewell.

MAR. Cruel one, why are you hiding the depths of your heart from me?

ER. Answer for me (*to* DECIO, *making him go into the middle*).

MAR. For all my sufferings, shall I never have pity?

DEC. Ask her (*sotto voce to* MARCELLO, *making him go into the middle*).

MAR. When will this sighing soul obtain peace?

ER. Aldimira knows.

MAR. Dear lively lips, tell me yes or no.

ER. Speak to her.

MAR. I do not wish pity from her, I wish pity from

Se la mia vita fei ,
Non mi negar mercè.
Non , &c.

SCENA XVII.

Eraclea , e Decio.

Er. E Pur tenta Marcello
L'invitta mia coftanza?
Dec. Lufinga degl'amanti è la fperanza.
Er. Ei fe fpera mercè, la fpera in vano;
Che nel mio petto amore
Con miracolo ftrano,
Per te gran fiáme in picciol tempo accefe.
Dec. E sì prefto il tuo core,
Tant'incendio per me deftar s'intefe?
Er. Fu l'ardente tuo fguardo,
Qual lampo che balena ,
E incenerifce al'or che tocca appena.
Dec. Quanto farei contento,
Se un intenfo tormento,
Con flagelli tiranni
Non turt affe il mio fen .
Er. Perche t'affanni?
Dec. Entro parte remota
Di tua Real Maggione,
Bramo renderti nota
Del'interno mio duol l'alta cagione.
Er Pago farai, ma intanto,
Col tuo dolor non invitarmi al pianto.
Dec Langue confufa, e mefta
L'anima mia,qualche fventura è quefta.
Er Cangia in ardir la tema ,
Scuoti lo fpirto oppreffo
Non far che l'alma gema,
Non effere a te fteffo
Prefago di fventure Idolo mio.

Dec.

Dec. Se così vuole il Ciel, che far pofs'io?
Er. Se il mio cor ti vive in petto
Non affliggere il tuo core ;
Habbia il tuo tutto il diletto ,
Habbia il mio tutto il dolore.
Se il, &c.

SCENA XVII.

Decio .

Che penfo? che rifolvo?
Quello fon io,che a la Città Latina
Per non mancar di fede
Seppi la mia foffrire alta rovina,
Ed ora io fono quello,
Che de'mirti d'amor cinto la chioma,
Son rivale a Marcello,e infido a Roma?
Cederò la mia vaga
Al gran Duce del Tebro,
Saprò tutto valore
Privarmi d'Eraclea: ma con qual core ?
Nel mio petto con fiera battaglia ,
Fanno guerra la gloria, e l'amore,
L'uno,e l'altra grã fulmini fcaglia;
Ma non sò di chi fia la vittoria ,
Sò che mai,ne l'amor,ne la gloria,
Non dã tregua al mio povero core.
Nel mio,&c.

Fine dell'Atto Secondo.

C 4

you. If you are my life, do not deny me mercy. I do not, etc.

Scene xvii
ERACLEA *and* DECIO
ER. And is Marcello still laying siege to my unconquered constancy?
DEC. Hope ever flatters lovers.
ER. If he hopes for mercy, he hopes in vain; for Love awakened in my bosom by a strange miracle a great flame for you in a short time.
DEC. And did your heart feel such great flames arise for me so quickly?
ER. It was your blazing gaze, like a bolt of lightning which flashes and reduces to ashes as soon as it barely touches.
DEC. How happy I would be, if an intense torment, with cruel lashes, did not disturb my bosom.
ER. Why are you troubled?
DEC. In a remote part of your royal palace, I desire to make known to you the deep reason for my inner unhappiness.
ER. You will be satisfied, but meanwhile do not make me weep with your sorrow.
DEC. My soul is pining, confused and sad; this is some misfortune.

ER. Change your fear into boldness and arouse your oppressed spirit. Do not make my spirit groan, do not be a harbinger of misfortune for yourself, my lord.
DEC. If Heaven wills it, what can I do?
ER. If my heart is living in your bosom, do not afflict your heart; let yours have all the happiness, let mine have all the sorrow. If my heart, etc.

Scene xvii[i]
DECIO
What can I think? What can I decide? I am the man who, in order not to be unfaithful to Rome, was able to bear up under the ruin of all my fortune; and now am I the man who, with his brow crowned with the myrtles of love, am a rival to Marcello and faithless to Rome? I shall yield my beloved to the great general of the Tiber; I shall be able, with bravery, to give up Eraclea, but with what kind of heart?
In my bosom, with a fierce struggle, glory and love are battling. Both are hurling great thunderbolts, but I do not know which will have the victory. I know that neither love nor glory ever gives my poor heart peace. In my, etc.

ATTO III.

SCENA PRIMA.

Mezzanini del Palazzo d'Eraclea, nei quali
abbita Decio.

Eraclea, e Decio.

Er. DEcio, Decio.
Dec. DE tu vieni
De le mie stanze ad onorar le foglie?
Scusa se in queste spoglie
A te Signora oso portarmi innante.
Er. Mosse l'anima amante
Sollecito desire,
D'intender l'aspro occulto tuo martire.
Dec. Tanto de tuoi, tanto de danni miei
Impaziente sei d'udir novella?
Er. (Numi che mai farà?) Siedi, e favella.
  si mettono a sede e.
Dec. Già tu sai quanto t'amo.
Er. E sai tu ancora,
  Quanto Eraclea t'adora.
Dec. Mai non haveste, oh Dio,
  L'amor tuo corrisposto al'amor mio.
Er. Perche?
Dec. Sarebbe, ahi lasso,
  Men tiranno per noi questo gran passo.
Er. Spiega l'infausta nova.
Dec. Medita l'alma i modi, e non li trova.
Er. Parla libero pure,
  Che io sono avvezza a sostener sventure.
Dec. E se poi le mie voci
  Ti sono al cor d'aspre punture atroci?
Er. Risolviti una volta,
  Petto bastante hò da sentirti.
Dec. Ascolta.

Son rival di Marcello,
E con esser di scherno agl'amor sui,
La sè giurata a Roma offendo in lui.
Er. Dunque?
Dec. Sanno gli Dei
  Se intrepido perdei,
  Quanto amica fortuna a me già diede,
  Per non contaminar sì bella fede.
Er. Ed or?
Dec. Perdona al giusto mio valore,
  Perder convien ciò che mi diede amore.
Er. Come?
Dec. Ceder ti deggio
  Al gran Duce del Tebro Idolo bello.
Er. Tu cedermi a Marcello?
  Ingannatore,
    Anima infida,
    Se oltraggi amore,
    Amor t'uccida.
  Ingannatore, &c.
Dec. Ti sovenga Eraclea,
  Che vanti un cor nel seno
  Da soffrir quante pene il Ciel t'appresta.
Er. Ho core sì, ma non hò cor per questa.
  Crudel, nel dì che nasce,
  Il mio tenero amor l'uccidi in fasce.
  Dimmi, che ti facemmo ed egli, ed io?
Dec. Eraclea.
Er. Decio.
a 2. Oh Dio.
Er. Vedi che tua già sono,
  Sgorga per te da questi lumi il pianto,
  Per te sospiro tanto,
  E l'alma tua comporta,
  Ch'io d'altri sia? non posso più son morta.
Dec. Deh l'angoscie raffrena,
  E la smania del senso
  Sia da forte ragione oppressa, e doma.

C 5   Er.

Son

ACT III

Scene i

Mezzanine of Eraclea's palace, in which Decio lives;
ER. and DEC.

ER. Decio, Decio!

DEC. Do you come to honor the threshold of my rooms? Excuse me if, in this garb, I dare to come into your presence, my lady.

ER. My loving heart was moved by concern to hear of your secret intense torment.

DEC. Are you so impatient to have word of your and my doom?

ER. O Gods, what can it possibly be? Sit, and speak. (They sit.)

DEC. You already know how much I love you.

ER. And you, too, know how much Eraclea adores you.

DEC. Oh, Heavens, that your love had never requited mine!

ER. Why?

DEC. This great step, alas, would have been less cruel for us.

ER. Explain this unauspicious news.

DEC. My soul is trying to find ways and cannot.

ER. Speak freely, for I am accustomed to suffer misfortunes.

DEC. And if my words come as sharp, cruel stabs to your heart?

ER. Gather your courage, for I have enough strength to listen to you.

DEC. Listen. I am Marcello's rival, and if I stand in the way of his love, I offend, in him, the faith which I have sworn to Rome.

ER. Well, then?

DEC. The Gods know whether I fearlessly lost everything that a friendly fortune had given me, so as not to sully so lofty a faith.

ER. And now?

DEC. Forgive my righteous courage; I must give up what Love gave me.

ER. What?

DEC. I must yield you to the great general of the Tiber, my idol.

ER. You, yield me to Marcello?
Deceiver, faithless soul, if you outrage Love, may Love kill you. Deceiver, etc.

DEC. Remember, Eraclea, that you boast a heart in your bosom which can suffer whatever troubles Heaven inflicts on you.

ER. I have a heart, yes, but I have no heart for this. Cruel one, on the day when it is born, you kill my tender love in its cradle. Tell me, what have he and I done to you?

DEC. Eraclea! }
ER. Decio! } (together) Oh Heavens!

ER. You see that I am already yours. Let tears flow for you from these eyes. I sigh so much for you, and your soul allows me to belong to someone else? I can bear it no longer; I am done for.

DEC. Ah, restrain your sorrow, and may the ravings of your feelings be repressed and conquered by the strength of reason.

Er. Serba l'amore a me, la fede a **Roma**.

Dec. Lafcio ad altri Eraclea,
    Ma lafciando Eraclea, non lafcio amore.

Er. Tu cedermi a Marcello? Ingannatore.

Dec. A perdita sì grave
    La gloria mia la gloria tua mi guida.

Er. Tu cedermi a Marcello? anima infida

Dec. Al fin fcoprir pur deve,
    Che Decio io fono, e che ti fono amate,
    E ch'ei per me gli fprezzi tuoi riceve,
    Onde a tuo fcorno, ed a vendetta mia,
    Ciò che gli cedo, egli rapir potria,
    Ed ofcurando ogni mio pregio antico,
    Sarei di me, farei di tè nemico.

Er. (Cieli foccorfo, aita,
    Quanto meglio faria perder la vita.)

Dec. (Che tormento.)

Er. (Che affanno.)

Dec. (Il mio feno trafigge.)

Er. (Opprime il mio.)

Dec. Eraclea.

Er. Decio.

a 2. Oh Dio.

Er. Troppo la forte in oltraggiarmi è fiera.

Dec. Ai colpi fuoi lo fpirto tuo non cada.

Er. Decio, trionfa, e vada
    La gloria tua de miei fofpiri altera,
    Lafcia chi tanto t'ama,
    E il mio duol fia trofeo de la tua fama.
    Godi ch'è fatto pago il tuo defio.

Dec. Eraclea.

Er. Decio.

a 2. Oh Dio.

Er. Tu cedimi a Marcello,
    Ma non lagnarti poi
    Se agl'amor fuoi vinta Eraclea non cede:
    Tu la tua vuoi ferbare, io la mia fede.

Dec. E s'egli d'ira cieco

               Tuo

Tuo nemico diviene,
Di fervili catene,
Se il piè ti cinge, e teco
Là nel Tarpeo con difpettofo vanto,
Le dolci figlie tue fi tragge accanto?

Er. Forfe non v'è per me ferro, o veleno?
    Forfe da quefto feno   *fe levano in piedi*
    Non sà l'anima forte,
    Ufcir fuperba ad incontrar la morte?

Dec. Difperato configlio.

Er. Par difperato, e del valore è figlio.
    Morrò pria di tradirti,
    E tu fpietato, lafciami infepolta;
    L'alma in fofpir difciolta,
    Andrà con alto grido,
    Efclamando così di lido in lido:
    Ombra fon d'Eraclea, che a Decio arrifi,
    Decio lafciommi, ed io per lui m'uccifi.
       Morir per te defio

Dec.   Deh non morir per me

a 2.   Idolo mio.

Er.   Saprò fvenarmi ancora
         Per non mancar di fè.

Dec.   Non bramo che tu mora,
         O vuò morire anch'io.

Er.   Morir, &c.

SCENA II.

Galleria.

Alfeo in abito di gala, e poi Lilla.

Alf. S'E cangiata in bizzaria,
    La mia foda gravità;
    Con moderna fimetria
    Si vestì l'antichità.
    S'è, &c.

     C 6   *Li.*

ER. Keep your love for me, and your faith for Rome.

DEC. I give up Eraclea to another, but, while I give up Eraclea, I do not give up my love.

ER. You give me up to Marcello? Deceiver!

DEC. He is bound to discover in the end that I am Decio, and your lover, and that he is the object of your scorn on my account; wherefore, for your shame, and for vengeance on me, what I am now yielding to him, he might take by force—and, blackening all my former reputation, I would be my enemy and yours.

ER. (Heavens, rescue me, aid me! How much better it would be to lose my life!)

DEC. (What torment!)

ER. (What torture!)

DEC. (It oppresses my bosom.)

ER. (It crushes mine.)

DEC. Eraclea!
        (together) Oh Heavens!
ER. Decio!

ER. Fate is too cruel in outraging me.

DEC. Do not let your spirit fall under its blows.

ER. Decio, be victorious, and let your glory be proud of my sighs. Abandon her who loves you so much, and let my sorrow be a trophy of your fame. Enjoy the satisfaction of your desires.

DEC. Eraclea!   } *(together)* Oh Heavens!
ER. Decio!   }

ER. Yield me to Marcello, but do not complain afterwards if Eraclea, conquered, does not yield to his love. You wish to save your glory, I my faithfulness.

DEC. And if he, blind with wrath, becomes your enemy; if he binds your feet with the chains of a slave and drags your sweet daughters alongside you, with contemptuous boasting, to the Tarpeian rock?

ER. Perhaps there is for me no sword or poison? *(They rise.)* Perhaps does my soul not know how to issue forth bravely from this bosom to meet death proudly?

DEC. This is a counsel of despair.

ER. It seems born of despair, but it is born of courage. I shall die before betraying you, and you, pitiless, leave me unburied. My soul, dissolved in sighs, will go from shore to shore, with loud cries, exclaiming "I am the shade of Eraclea, who smiled on Decio; Decio abandoned me, and I killed myself for him." I wish to die for you . . .   }*(together)* . . . my
DEC. O do not die for me . . . }idol.

ER. I shall open my veins, so as not to be unfaithful.

DEC. I do not wish you to die, or else I wish to die as well.

ER. I wish, etc.

Scene ii
Gallery; ALFEO *in gala costume, and later* LILLA.

AL. My solid gravity has changed to eccentricity. Let antiquity be garbed in modern symmetry. My solid, etc.

Li. (Che veggio! queſto è Alfeo! che Vecchio
Serva Signor Dottore. (ſtolto.)

Alf. Bella Ragazza addio.

Li. Mi piaci molto,
Col peruccone, e con il giuſtacore.

Alf. Mi ſon veſtito al'uſo, e ſotto, e ſopra
Sol per la tua bellezza.

Li. Queſta è troppa finezza, ella ſi copra.
Or vorrei caro Alfeo,
Saper ſe tu ſai far da Cicisbeo.

Alf. Non vi ſon coſe nuove
Per un che tanto sà.

Li. Dunque a le prove.

Alf. Oſſerva che maniera agile, e deſtra.

Li. Figurati vedermi a la fineſtra.

Fanno molti atti muti amoreggiando tra loro.
Bravo aſſai.

Alf. Che ti pare?
Tutto ſan fare le perſone dotte.

Li. Or figurati tù che ſia di notte.
tornano ad amoreggiare.

Alf. Bene ti par che vada?

Li. Sì. Fingi adeſſo d'incontrarmi in ſtrada.
Come ſopra.

Alf. Dimmela giuſta, in far da vago ſceglio,
Gl'atti più proprii?

Li. Non ſi può far meglio.

Alf. Mi comanda la ſorte,
Ch'io ſia lo ſpoſo tuo.

Li. Tu mio conſorte?

Alf. Ci hai repugnanza alcuna?

Li. Anzi è mia gran fortuna,
Perche ſera, e matina
Sotto la tua dottrina
Diſciplinata Lilla,
Un giorno ſverrà ſavia Sibilla.

Alf. Sarai dotta, ſagace,
In pochi dì, perche tu ſei capace.

Mà

Mà gioja mia quando farem tra noi
Le nozze che deſio?

Li. Quando tu vuoi.

Alf. Adeſſo

Li. Flemma, flemma,
Dammi un tantin di tempo.

Alf. Sbrigati mio teſoro,
Più preſto che tu puoi perche mi moro.

Li. Dunque per me tu ſenti.

Alf. Diluvii di tormenti,
Non hò un ora di bene,
E degli affanni miei, chi và, chi viene.

Li. Decrepito Adone,
T'hò pur compaſſione.

Alf. Lilletta Lilletta,
Che ſii benedetta.

Li. Son
Alf. Sei } *a 2* tutta pietà.

Li. Ti prendo la mano,
E ſtretta la tengo

Alf. Pian piano, pian piano,
Già ſento che ſvengo.

Li. Stà lieto, ſtà lieto.

Alf. Deh piglia l'aceto,
Che Alfeo ſe ne và.
Decrepito, &c.

SCENA III.

Irene, e Flavia.

Fla. (Giurar fede ad Iliſo?)

Ir. (Mancare al primo amore?)

Fla. (Anima ſconſigliata.)

Ir. (Incauto core.)

Fla. (Prendere a gioco Irene?)

Ir. (Schernir la mia Germana?)

Fla. (Ed io ſon tanto infana?)

C 7

Ir.

LI. (What do I see! That is Alfeo! What a silly old man!) Your servant, Doctor.

AL. Fair damsel, greetings.

LI. I like you very much with a big wig and doublet.

AL. I have dressed according to fashion, top and bottom, just on account of your beauty.

LI. This is too much elegance; put on your hat. Now I would like to know, dear Alfeo, if you can be a gigolo.

AL. There are no novelties for one who knows as much as I do.

LI. Then, to the test.

AL. Observe what agile and skillful ways I have.

LI. Imagine you are seeing me at the window.

(They make a great deal of dumb show of love-making between them.)

LI. Very good indeed!

AL. What do you think? Learned persons know how to do everything.

LI. Now imagine it's nighttime.

(More dumb show of love-making.)

AL. Well, do you think it's all right?

LI. Yes. Now make believe you are meeting me on the street.

(As above.)

AL. Tell me truly, am I choosing the most fitting gestures as a lover?

LI. You couldn't do any better.

AL. Fate commands that I should be your bridegroom.

LI. You, my husband?

AL. Does the idea still repel you?

LI. On the contrary, it is great good luck for me, be-

cause night and day, under your teachings, Lilla will become learned and will one day be a wise Sybil.

AL. You will be learned and wise in a few days, because you are able. My jewel, when will we have the wedding that I desire?

LI. When you wish.

AL. Now.

LI. Take it easy, take it easy. Give me a little time.

AL. Hurry up, my beloved, as quickly as possible, for I am dying.

LI. So you feel for me . . .

AL. Floods of torments. I have not a single hour of repose, and my troubles come and go.

LI. Decrepit Adonis, I feel pity for you.

AL. Lilletta, Lilletta, blessings on you.

LI. I am
AL. You are } *(together)* all pity.

LI. I take your hand, and hold it tightly.

AL. Softly, softly, I already feel I am fainting.

LI. Be happy, be happy.

AL. My smelling salts, for Alfeo is swooning.
Decrepit, etc.

Scene iii
IRENE *and* FLAVIA

FL. (Swear faithfulness to Iliso?)

IR. (Be untrue to my first love?)

FL. (Ill-advised soul!)

IR. (Heedless heart!)

FL. (Mock Irene?)

IR. (Scorn my sister?)

FL. (And am I so base?)

Ir. (Ah non conviene.)
Fla. (Mi ribello a Damiro?)
Ir. (A Damiro mi dono?)
Fla. (Forfennata deliro.)
Ir. (E ftolta io fono.)
Fla. Irene.
Ir. Flavia mia.
Fla. Del mio grave ardimento.
Ir. Di mia ceca follia.
Fla. Io ti chieggio perdono.
Ir. Ed'io mi pento.
Fla. Ti ftringo al fen.
Ir. T'abbraccio.
Fla. Torno al' antico laccio.
Ir. Al primo foco afpiro.
Fla. Lafcio Ilifo per te.
Ir. Per te Damiro.

    Amor che forte impiaga,
      Che fpeffo in noi fi defta,
      E folo il primo amor.
      Tal'or la prima piaga,
      Si fana è ver, ma refta
      La cicatrice al cor.
    Amor, &c.

S C E N A IV.

Ilifo, e Flavia.

Il. FLavia, Flavia mio bene.
Fla. Non dire a me così, dillo ad Irene
Il. Meco fcherzando vai.
Fla. Non fcherzo già.
Il. Perche?
Fla. Ti niego quella fè che ti giurai.
Il. Troppo manchi a te fteffa.
Fla. E'vana la promeffa,
    Che ti feci in amore:

                   Non

    Non era in sè, ma vaneggiava il core.
Il. Cor del tuo più leggiero,
    Cor del mio più fchernito ove fi diede?
    Son deftinato a non trovar mai fede.
Fla. Vanne, foffri, e datti pace.
      Sono amante,
       D'un fembiante,
      Che mi piacque, e che mi piace.
    Vanne......
Il. Refta fpergiura, empia, fallace.   *part*
Fla. Vanne, foffri, e datti pace.

S C E N A V.

Flavia.

PArte dal mare il rivo,
   E fcorrendo fen và con onde chiare,
   E prati, e bofchi, e poi ritorna al mare;
   Qual Rufcello fon'io,
   Parto, e poi fò ritorno al Idol mio.
   Vuò che Damiro folo,
   Degl'eterni amor miei l'oggetto fa;
   Chi sà che al mio morir vita non dia?
     Farfalletta, che amante deliro,
      Non fofpiro,
      Che il dolce mio lume.
     Voglio tanto girargli d'intorno,
     Fin che un giorno,
     Pietà fenta del'arfe mie piume.
   Farfalletta, &c.

S C E N A VI.

Decio, Livio, e poi Marcello.

Dec. LIvio non è più tempo
    Di mentir feffo, fpogliati di quefti
   Feminili ornamenti, e i tuoi rivefti.

                   Li.

IR. (Ah, it should not be so.)
FL. (Shall I abandon Damiro?)
IR. (Shall I give myself to Damiro?)
FL. (I am raving mad.)
IR. (And I am foolish.)
FL. Irene . . .
IR. My Flavia . . .
FL. . . . for my wicked daring . . .
IR. . . . for my blind folly . . .
FL. . . . I beg you to pardon me.
IR. . . . I repent.
FL. I press you to my bosom.
IR. I embrace you.
FL. I shall return to my first attachment.
IR. I long for my first love.
FL. I leave Iliso for you . . .
IR. . . . and Damiro for you.

That love which deeply wounds, which often arises in us, is only the first love. On occasion the first wound heals, 'tis true, but the scar remains in the heart. That love, etc.

Scene iv
ILISO *and* FLAVIA

IL. Flavia, my beloved!
FL. Don't say that to me, say it to Irene.
IL. You're joking with me.
FL. I'm not joking.
IL. Why?
FL. I deny you that faith which I swore to you.

IL. You are too unfaithful to yourself.
FL. The promise of love which I made you is vain; my heart was not sane, but was wandering irresponsibly.
IL. Where was there ever a heart more irresponsible than yours, more scorned than mine? I am fated never to find true faith.
FL. Go, suffer, and find peace. I am in love with a face which pleased me and which still pleases me. Go, suffer, etc.
IL. Remain, perjured one, impious one, deceitful one. *(Exit.)*
FL. Go, suffer, and find peace.

Scene v
FLAVIA

The river leaves the sea and runs with clear waters past fields and woods, and then returns to the sea. I am like a brook: I leave, and then I return to my idol. I want only Damiro to be the object of my eternal love. Who knows but that he will give life to my dying?

Like a moth, delirious with love, I am sighing only for my beloved flame. I wish to flutter around him, until one day he will feel pity for my singed wings. Like a moth, etc.

Scene vi
DECIO, LIVIO, *and later* MARCELLO

DEC. Livio, it is time to conceal our sex no longer. Take off those feminine clothes and put on your own.

Dunque mi dia licenza,
Che anderò per servir vostra Eccellenza.
Dec. Vanne, ma cauto cela,
Chi sei tu, chi son'io,
In sino che il labro mio non lo rivela:
Li. Il mio giudizio adopro,
E se tu nó ti scoprìio non mi scopro. *parte.*
Mar. Aldimira.
Dec. Marcello.
Mar. Pace sperar mi lice?
Dec. La novella è gioconda,
Mar. O me felice.
Dec. Il Cavaliere amante
Le mie preghiere intese
Turbossi al primo istante, e poi si rese:
Mà con qual duolo immenso,
Ahi che mi reca orrore, or che vi penso.
Mar. Gran forza hanno i tuoi voti.
Dec. Anzi il tuo nome.
Mar. Come Aldimira come?
Dec. Ei con eroica fede,
Morir si sente, ed Eraclea ti cede.
Mar. Cavalier sì gentil chi sia ti chieggio.
Dec. Non cercar più, ch'ora più dir nó deggio.
Mar. E vuoi, che à me sia dato
Il vilissimo titolo d'ingrato?
Dec. Non guari andrà, che innante
Meco faprò guidarlo al tuo sembiante.
Mar. Me'l prometti.
Dec. Il vedrai.
Mar. Quanto ti deggio, ò quanto.
Dec. S'io per te feci tanto,
Tu per me che farai?
Mar. Quello che brami, e prego,
Che mi fulmini il Ciel, se à te lo nego.
Dec. Senti se chiedo affai
Tal'or, quando Eraclea ti stringi in braccio
Ricordale, ch'io l'amo, e servo, e taccio.
Mar.

Mar. Poco chiede
La tua fede
à 2. Per mercè d'un tanto amor.
Dec. Più non chiede
La mia fede
Per mercè d'un tanto amor.
Mar. Altra pace altro sollievo
Tu non vuoi? Dec. Voler non devo.
Mar. E ti basta sol così?
Dec. Basta sì, di più non bramo,
Sol ricordale ch'io l'amo,
E che servo, e taccio ancor.
Poco, &c.

SCENA VII.

Decio.

Dec. CHi sà forse Eraclea
Di Marcello Conforte,
Andrà del Tebro in sù le belle arene
A me restar conviene
Onde de la mia perdita m'attristo
Non già del suo così felice acquisto
Vanto un amor ch'ogn'altro amore eccede,
Mà più di questo amor grande è la fede.
Già mai la lontananza
Farà dal'alma mia
Svanir sì dolce amor,
E l'altá mia costanza
Non mancherà se pria
In me non manca il cor'.

SCE-

LI. Then grant me leave, and I will go and obey your Excellency.

DEC. Go, but be cautious and conceal who you are, and who I am, until my lips reveal it.

LI. I shall use my judgment, and if you do not reveal yourself, I shall not reveal myself. *(Exit.)*

MAR. Aldimira!

DEC. Marcello!

MAR. Can I hope for peace?

DEC. The answer is favorable.

MAR. Happy me!

DEC. The knight, her lover, on hearing my request was at first upset, and then yielded; but with such intense sorrow that, alas, it horrifies me to think of it!

MAR. Your wishes have great force.

DEC. Nay, rather, your name.

MAR. What, Aldimira, what?

DEC. He, with heroic faith, feels himself dying, and yields Eraclea to you.

MAR. Who such a noble knight may be, I beg you tell me.

DEC. Do not ask any more, for I may now say nothing further.

MAR. And do you want me to be given the base name of an ingrate?

DEC. It will not be long before I shall bring him with me into your presence.

MAR. Promise me.

DEC. You shall see him.

MAR. How much am I indebted to you, O how much!

DEC. If I have done so much for you, what will you do for me?

MAR. Whatever you wish, and I pray that Heaven may strike me with thunderbolts if I refuse you.

DEC. See if I am asking enough: on occasion, when you embrace Eraclea, remind her that I love her, serve, and am silent.

MAR. Your faith asks but little } *(together)* as
DEC. My faith asks nothing more } reward for so great a love.

MAR. Do you wish no other token of peace, no other relief?

DEC. I may not wish it.

MAR. And is just this enough?

DEC. It is enough; nothing more do I desire. Only remind her that I love her, and that I serve, and am still silent. Your faith asks, etc.

Scene vii
DECIO

Who knows, perhaps Eraclea will go as Marcello's bride to the fair sands of the Tiber. I must remain where I grieve over my loss. A love which surpasses all other loves does not boast of its happy gain; but greater than even this love, is faith.
Never will distance make such a sweet love vanish from my heart, and my exalted faithfulness will perish in me only when my heart perishes. Never will, etc.

S C E N A VIII.

Irene, poi Ilifo, poi Damiro in difparte.

Ir. **P**Iù non voglio amarne tanti
    Voglio amare un volto fol
    Che l'andar cangiando amanti
    E'un cangiar duolo per duol.
      Più, &c.
Ir. Ilifo e creder puoi,
Ch'abbia al mio labro acconfentito il core?
Per prova del tuo amore
Seguir finfi Damiro
Fù doppio ogni fofpiro
Mentii gli fcherni à tuo difprezzo, e vera
Non fù la fiamma mia.
Il. (Che menfognera?)
Ir. Mà volubile amante
    Tu fubito mi fdegni,e Flavia adori:
O miei poveri amori!
Alma tanto incoftante
Serbi nel petto?ah che infedel fei tu,
Tal non è Irene tua.
Il. (Quefto di più?)
Ire. Pure il genio mi tragge
    A fempre amarti,e vita mia ti chiamo,
E del'infedeltà t'affolvo, e t'amo.
Dam. (T'amo! che udii?)   *in difparte.*
Il. Non curo
Gl'amori tuoi .
Ire. Spergiuro,
    Vedi fe infido fei.
Dam. (Soccorretemi ò Dei.)
Ire. E il mio fiero cordoglio
    Non ti move à pietà?

                  Il.

Il. Più non ti voglio.
Ir. Deh caro Ilifo al mio voler compiaci.
Dam. (Alma rea.)
Ir. Sarò tua.
Il. Più non mi piaci .

S C E N A IX.

Damiro, e Irene.

Dam. **L**A tua forta mi 'duole   (vuole
    Più non gli piaci nò , più non ti
Incoftante l u finghiera
Cangia core, ò cangia volto
Menfognera . . . . . .
Eh che fon ftolto.
Ad ordir tradimenti
Troppo avvezza tu fei.   *vuol partire.*
Ire. Damiro fenti
    Se mai non è l'iftesso
    Quel ben che il cor defia
    E'mia fatalità .
    Come fi cangi fpesso
    La fiamma, che m'accende
    Queft'alma non l'intende
    Irene non lo sà .
    Se mai, &c.

S C E N A X.

Flavia, Damiro.

Fla. **C**Aro Damiro ò quanto
    Del'incoftanza fua Flavia s'affligge
Ecco mi ftruggo in pianto,
Tutta pentita io fono ,
E ti chieggio pietà non che perdono.
Dam. Suol de le donne il petto

                    D'

Scene viii
IRENE, *and later* ILISO *and* DAMIRO *to one side*

IR. I no longer wish to love so many, I wish to love one alone; for continually changing lovers is exchanging one sorrow for another. I no longer, etc.

IR. Iliso, can you believe that my heart has agreed with my lips? To test your love, I pretended to favor Damiro. Each sigh was false; I scorned and despised you falsely, and my love for him was not true.

IL. (What a liar!)

IR. But you, a fickle lover, immediately disdained me, and you adore Flavia. O unhappy love of mine! Have you such an inconstant heart in your bosom? Ah, even if you are faithless, your Irene is not.

IL. (This, too!)

IR. Yet my spirit brings me to love you always, and I call you my life, and I forgive you for your faithlessness, and I love you.

DAM. ("I love you!" What have I heard?)

IL. I care nothing for your love.

IR. Perjurer, see whether you are faithless.

DAM. (Help me, O Gods!)

IR. And does my fierce torment not move you to pity?

IL. I desire you no longer.

IR. Ah, dear Iliso, do as I desire.

DAM. (Wicked soul!)

IR. I shall be yours.

IL. I don't like you any longer.

Scene ix
DAMIRO *and* IRENE

DAM. Your fate moves me to pity. He doesn't like you, doesn't want you any longer. Inconstant, flatterer, change your heart or change your face, liar . . . Ah, how foolish I am! You are too much given to plotting betrayals. *(starts to exit)*

IR. Damiro, listen!
If that treasure which the heart desires is not ever the same, it is my fate. How the flame which enkindles me changes so often, I do not understand, Irene does not know. If, etc.

Scene x
FLAVIA *and* DAMIRO

FL. Beloved Damiro, O how much Flavia regrets her inconstancy. Behold, I am dissolved in tears. I am all repentant, and I beg you for pity as well as for pardon.

DAM. Woman's bosom is usually the nesting place of

D'infedeltà vagante effere il nido:
Veggio gl'affanni tuoi, mà non mi fido.

Fla. Ben mio fe à me non credi
Ecco il feno di Flavia, aprilo, e vedi.

Dam (Per oltraggio d'Irene
Amerò Flavia, e fia
La traditrice mia da me tradita,
Refti così l'infedeltà punita.)

Fla. Teco fteffo che parli?

Dam. Eterna fede
Se in te trovar fperaffi io t'amerei.

Fla. Amami, e non temer degl' amor miei,
Che rifpondi?

Dam. Confento
Al tuo defio.

Fla. Tutta bear mi fento.

Dam. Mà qual pregio in me trovi
Onde ad amarmi, ed à languir ti movi?

Fla. Quegl'occhi oh Dio quegl'occhi
San dare certi fguardi,
Ch'efprimere non sò
Quanto rapifcono.
E con tal gratia fcocchi
Dal tuo bel ciglio i dardi,
Che ridir non fi può
Come ferifcono.
Quegl'occhi, &c.

S C E N A   XI.

Damiro.

ARdo per Flavia, e quanto
Irene prima amai, l'odio altrettanto.
Amor non trova un core
Se non hà fedeltà;
E fe pur trova amore,
E amor che dura poco,

E che

E che di fdegno al foco
Odio tal'or fi fà.
Amor, &c.

S C E N A   XII.

Marcello, & Eraclea.

Mar. E Pur fei tanto fiera?

Er. Dunque pietà difpera.

Mar. Eraclea ti rammento,
Che Aldimira può far, ch'io fia contento.

Er. Ogni fpeme difcaccia.

Mar. E s'ella il fà.

Er. Non crederò, che il faccia.

Mar. E fe il faceffe, e che diretti al'ora.

Er. Oh Dio non più, creder nol poffo ancora.

Mar. Bei labri adorati
Direte di sì
Non fempre fpietati
Sarete così.
Bei labri, &c.

S C E N A   XIII.

Eraclea, poi Alfeo, e poi Flavia, ed Irene.

Er. O Là

Alf. Per obedirti Alfeo qui viene.

Fr. Voglio Flavia, ed Irene.

Alf. Or le chiamo.   *parte.*

Er. Eraclea
E' vicino il periglio,
Generofo configlio
Vuol che più tofto io mora.

Fl. Principeffa.

Ir. Signora.

Er. A i miei feroci accenti

Non

---

wandering faithlessness; I see your trouble, but I don't trust you.

FL. My beloved, if you don't believe me, here is Flavia's heart; open it and see.

DAM. (To get revenge on Irene, I shall love Flavia, and my betrayer will be betrayed by me; may faithlessness be punished in this way.)

FL. What are you saying to yourself?

DAM. If I hoped to find eternal faith in you, I would love you.

FL. Love me, and do not fear for my love. What do you answer?

DAM. I will satisfy your desire.

FL. I feel entirely happy.

DAM. But what merit do you find in me? Why do you decide to love me and pine for me?

FL. Those eyes, O Heavens, those eyes can give certain glances, so that I cannot express how much they enrapture me; and you shoot from your fair eyes such arrows that it is impossible to tell how they wound. Those eyes, etc.

Scene xi
DAMIRO

I am in love with Flavia, and, as much as I loved Irene before, I now hate her fully as much.

A heart does not find love unless it has faithfulness; and if indeed it does find love, it is a short-lived

love, and one which, in the fire of disdain, often becomes hatred. A heart does not find love, etc.

Scene xii
MARCELLO *and* ERACLEA

MAR. And are you still so hostile?

ER. Therefore give up hope of pity.

MAR. Eraclea, I remind you that Aldimira can bring happiness about for me.

ER. Abandon all hope.

MAR. And if she does so?

ER. I do not think that she will do so.

MAR. And if she did, what would you say then?

ER. Oh, Heavens, no more, I still cannot believe it!

MAR. Fair adored lips, say yes; you will not always be so pitiless. Fair lips, etc.

Scene xiii
ERACLEA, *then* ALFEO *then* FLAVIA *and* IRENE

ER. Ho there!

AL. Alfeo comes here to obey you.

ER. I want Flavia and Irene.

AL. I shall call them now. (*Exit.*)

ER. Eraclea, danger is near; the demand of nobility is that I rather die.

FL. Princess!

IR. My lady!

ER. Let your hearts not be dismayed in your bosoms

Non si sgomenti il vostro core in seno
    Cava un piccolo vaso.
Figlie questo è veleno.
Se mai vuole Marcello
Render per pompa sua per nostro scorno
Di me di voi il suo trionfo adorno,
Non patirò d'esser mostrata à dito
Da la Plebe Romana in Campidoglio.
Fl. Che farem?   *à Iren.*
Ir. Che farai?   *ad Erac.*
Er. Morire io voglio.
Fl. Genitrice.
Ir. Eraclea.
Er. Non hò cor, non hò ardire
    Da invitarvi à morire,
    Perche mie figlie siete,
    Mà poi sò ben con qual rossor vivrete.
Ir. Sorte rea.
Fl. Crudo fato.
Er. Dan segno di viltà le vostre pene.
Fl.
Ir. } *à 2.* Ah Madre.
Er. Ascolta Flavia, ascolta Irene,
    Poiche sarà quest'alma
    Sciolta da suoi legami
    Sapete, che desio?
Fl. Che vuoi?
Ir. Che brami?
Er.   Queste pupille almeno
      Viscere del mio seno
      Al'or chiudete.
      E al freddo busto accanto
      Tutto cangiato in pianto
      Il latte, che vi diedi à me rendete.
Queste, &c.

SCE

SCENA XIV.

Damiro da una parte, e Iliso dall' altra.

Dam. Flavia.
Ilis. Irene.
Dam. Sì mesta?
Ilis. (Pietà ne sento.)
Dam. E che gran doglia è questa?
Ilis. Forse de' miei disprezzi
    La memoria t'affanna?
Dam. Se di me temi, il tuo timor t'inganna.
Ilis. Consolati ben mio,
    Che t'amerò.
Dam. Sai, che già tuo son'io.
Ilis. Il ciglio rasserena.
Dam. Cessino i pianti tuoi.
Fla. Che duol!
Ire. Che pena!
Dam. Qual dolor
Ilis. Qual martire
Dam. Ti sforza à lagrimar?
Ilis. Ti fà languire?
Dam. Deh parla. *Ilis.* Rispondi.
Fla. Non posso. *Ir.* Non sò.
Dam. Se il male nascondi
Il. } *a 2* Sanar non si può.
    Deh, &c.

SCENA XV.

Livio in habito d'uomo, e poi Alfeo.

Li. Ecco quì che da Campagna
    S'è vestito il Dio bambino,
    Buona gratia m'accompagna,
              Lin-

---

at my frightful words. *(takes out a little phial)* Daughters, this is poison. If Marcello ever wants to adorn his triumph with me and with you, for his glory and for our disgrace, I shall not endure being pointed out on the Capitol by the Roman mob.
FL. What shall we do? *(to* IRENE*)*
IR. What will you do? *(to* ERACLEA*)*
ER. I am determined to die.
FL. Mother!
IR. Eraclea!
ER. I have neither the heart nor the boldness to ask you to die, because you are my daughters; but I know full well with what shame you will remain alive.
IR. Wicked destiny!
FL. Cruel fate!
ER. Your unhappiness is evidence of baseness.
FL.
IR. } *(together)* Ah, Mother!
ER. Listen, Flavia; listen, Irene; since this soul will be freed from its bondage, do you know what I wish?
FL. What do you want?
IR. What do you desire?
ER. These eyes, at least, O offspring of my womb, then close; and beside my lifeless corpse, give me back the milk I gave you, all changed into tears. These, etc.

Scene xiv
DAMIRO *from one side and* ILISO *from the other*
DAM. Flavia!
IL. Irene!
DAM. So sad?
IL. (I feel pity for him.)
DAM. And what great sorrow is this?
IL. Perhaps does the memory of my contempt trouble you?
DAM. If you are afraid on my account, your fear deceives you.
IL. Console yourself, my treasure, for I shall love you.
DAM. You know that I am already yours.
IL. Recover your serenity.
DAM. Let your weeping cease.
FL. What pain!
IR. What torment!
FL. What pain . . .
IL. What sorrow . . .
DAM. . . . forces you to weep?
IL. . . . makes you repine?
DAM. Ah, speak!   IL. Answer!
FL. I cannot!   IR. I do not know how to!
DAM.
IL. } *(together)* If you conceal your trouble it cannot be remedied. Ah, etc.

Scene xv
LIVIO *in men's clothes, and later* ALFEO
LI. Behold, here the child god has dressed himself as a Neapolitan; good grace accompanies me, handsome

Lindo,e fnello ,
Fò da bello,
Ma però non c'è un quattrino.
Ecco, &c.

Alf. (E Lilla,o non è Lilla,
Forfe mi s'è abbagliata,
L'una,e l'altra pupilla?
E Lilla, ò non è Lilla.)

Li. (Ecco Alfeo ci hò pur gufto.)

Alf. Lilla perche non vai con vefta,e bufto?

Li. Che Lilla?con chi l'hai?

Alf. Se tu Lilla non fei ,
Ti raflomigli tutto quanto a lei,
E per la fimiglianza ,
Ch'hai con la fua fembianza,
Un genio di giovarti mi trafporta.

Li. Giuro che non fon Lilla .

Alf. Non importa.
Perche il Cielo ti fè fimile a quella
La tua fortuna invidio.

Li. Però quella non fon .

Alf. Non dà faftidio.
Sappi ch'io fon Dottore .

Li. Padron mio fervitore.

Alf. Havrai più volte intefo nominare,
Il Sig. Don Alfeo.

Li. Sì sì mi pare ,

Alf. Sotto di me che fon perito, e faggio,
Farefti negli ftudii un gran paffaggio.
Spiegami il tuo penfiero .

Li. Io per fcoprirti il vero ,
Mi diletto un tantin di Poefia.

Alf. Male .

Li. Perche ?

Alf. Devia
Dagl'altri ftudii,e neceffarii,e gravi.

Li. Perche fono men dolci,e men foavi .

Alf. E tu Lilla non fei ?

Li.

Li. E tu pur canti;
Non fono Lilla .

Alf. Avanti .

Li. Cerco di farmi pratico ,
E nel intreccio,e ne lo ftil Dramatico.

Alf. Peggio figliuolo , peggio .
Simil componimento ,
In faccia a cento, e cento
Si fuol rapprefentare,
Ogn'un vuol cenfurare,
Tanto chi non ne sà,quanto chi intende.

Li. Quefto è pan che fi rende.
Speffo per gioco anch'io,
Con qualche fatiretta,
Vado facendo un taglio a la baffetta.

Alf. E poffibile mai ,
Che tu Lilla non fia?

Li. T'inganni affai.

Alf. Sei Lilla , fei Lilla .
Sù dilla,sù dilla.

Li. Ti dico di nò

Alf. Sei quella , fei quella ,
Favella favella .

Li. Più dire non vuò .

Alf. Sei effa , fei effa .
Confeffa, confeffa.

Li. Di più non dirò .
Sei Lilla,&c.

S C E N A XVI.

Tempio di tutti gli Dei .

Decio, e poi Eraclea, poi Marcello,e poi tutti.

Dec. VOi del Cielo o Dei potenti,
Sò, che tutti amor fentite;
Per pietà de miei tormenti,
La

---

and slender. I act like a fine fellow, but there's not a penny in it. Behold, etc.

AL. (Is it Lilla or is it not Lilla? Perhaps have my eyes become dazzled? Is it Lilla, or is it not Lilla?)

LI. (Here is Alfeo. I'm really enjoying this.)

AL. Lilla, why are you not dressed in skirt and bodice?

LI. What Lilla? Who are you talking to?

AL. If you are not Lilla, you look absolutely like her; and for the resemblance which you bear to her appearance, a desire to be of use to you transports me.

LI. I swear that I am not Lilla.

AL. No matter. Because Heaven made you like her, I envy your good fortune.

LI. But I am not her.

AL. Don't be difficult. Know that I am a doctor.

LI. Master, at your service.

AL. You must have heard my name mentioned often: Dr. Alfeo.

LI. Yes, yes, I think I have.

AL. Under me, who am experienced and wise, you would make great progress in your studies. Tell me what you are thinking of.

LI. To tell you the truth, I take a certain amount of pleasure in poetry.

AL. That's bad.

LI. Why?

AL. It takes your mind off of other studies which are essential and serious.

LI. Because they are not so sweet and enjoyable.

AL. Are you not Lilla?

LI. Talk all you want, I am not Lilla.

AL. Go on.

LI. I am trying to become skilled in plot-making and in dramatic style.

AL. Even worse, my boy, even worse. They act compositions like this in the presence of hundreds and hundreds. Everyone wants to criticize, both those who know nothing about it and those who do know something.

LI. Here one can give back as good as one gets. I, too, often, for sport with some little satire, cut the cards.

AL. Is it really possible that you are not Lilla?

LI. You're quite mistaken.

AL. You're Lilla, you're Lilla. Come on, admit it, come on, admit it.

LI. I tell you, I'm not.

AL. You are she, you are she, speak, speak.

LI. I won't say anything more.

AL. You are she, you are she, confess, confess.

LI. I won't say anything more.

AL. You're Lilla, etc.

Scene xvi
Temple of all the Gods; DECIO, *then* ERACLEA, *then* MARCELLO, *then all.*

DEC. O ye all-powerful Gods in Heaven, I know that you all feel love; out of pity for my misery, have

La mia forte compatite.
Voi,&c.
Er O de pensieri miei,
Tormentoso pensier Decio inumano!
Sconoscente, che sei,
Farmi penar,farmi languire in vano,
Dec. Deh più non tormentarmi.
Er Ed hai cor di lasciarmi?
Ingratissimo mio dolce ribello,
Sai pur,che per te vivo.
Dec. Giunge Marcello.
Er Abbominato arrivo.
Mar. Se tu bella Eraclea,
Mortal non sembri al volto ed ai costumi,
Qui nel Tempio de Numi,
T'abbraccierò sposa,non men che Dea.
Er Che al mio seno io ti stringa?
Perdonami Signore
Del tuo credulo core è una lusinga.
Mar. Più schivarmi non puoi.
Fl Sommo Eroe degli Eroi.
Ir. Pari al tuo gran valor sia la pietade.
Fl. Per le Romulee strade.
Ir. Non condurre in catena ed ella,e noi.
Dec. Come?
Mar. Di che temete?
Ir.
Fla. a 2. Paventiam d'Eraclea.
Er. Figlie tacete.
Mar. Nasce da vil sospetto il vostro affanno
Son vincitore, ma non son tiranno.
Dam. O degno d'alta Istoria,e d'alti carmi.
Il. Degno d'essere inciso in brozi,e in marmi
Mar. Amici, andranno in faccia degli Dei,
Oggi i vostri sponsali uniti ai miei.
Eraclea già dicesti,
Che il tuo voler soggiace,
D'Aldimira il voler;Dimmi Aldimira,
Ch'ella

Ch'ella sia mia consenti?
Dec. (O Stelle!)
Er. (Che dirà?)
Dec. Io consento.
Er. Io non già.
Mar. Perche ti penti?
Manchi a te,manchi a lei,
E troppo sei del mio piacer nemica.
Er. Se manco ad Aldimira,ella te'l dica:
Quando Aldimira fosse,
Chi dispone così de voler miei,
Al'ora ad Aldimira io mancherei.
Marc. Tu che rispondi? a Decio.
Dec. Eccoti scorto innante,
Il Cavaliere amante,
Ecco Eraclea ti dono,
Mi credesti Aldimira, e Decio io sono,
Decio, che fido a Roma,
Nel Volturno natio
Macchiar non vuole il suo costante onore
E ch'ora in Eraclea ti cede il core.
Fla.
Dam. a 2. Che intendo mai?
Il.
Ir. a 2. Che sento?
Alf. Inaspettato evento.
Mar. Decio troppo ti deve
Il Romano Senato,
E a la tua fè non è Marcello ingrato.
Generosa ragione,
Fà che intrepida l'alma,
Su'l tumulto de'sensi erga la palma.
Resti lieta,e felice,
La fè di Decio, e d'Eraclea l'amore,
E se questa è il tuo cor,ti rendo il core.
Dec. O de la fede mia mercè gradita!
Er. A lui rendesti il core,a me la vita.
Il. Principessa deh sia,
Sposa

mercy on my fate. O ye, etc.

ER. O inhuman Decio, tormenting worry of my thoughts! Ingrate that you are, making me be miserable and pine in vain.

DEC. Ah, do not torment me any longer.

ER. And have you the heart to abandon me? My most ungrateful sweet rebel, you know that I live for you.

DEC. Here comes Marcello!

ER. I loathe his approach!

MAR. If you, beautiful Eraclea, do not seem mortal by your face and bearing, here in the Temple of the Gods I embrace you as my bride and as my goddess.

ER. That I should press you to my bosom? Forgive me, my lord, this is a deceit of your credulous heart.

MAR. You cannot escape any more.

FL. O great hero of heroes!

IR. Let your pity be equal to your great bravery.

FL. Through the streets of Rome . . .

IR. . . . do not lead her and us in chains.

DEC. What?

IR.
FL. }(together) We are afraid for Eraclea.

ER. Daughters, keep silent.

MAR. Your worry arises from a needless fear. I am a conqueror, but not a tyrant.

DAM. O man worthy of exalted history and of lofty song!

IL. Worthy of being sculptured in bronze and marble!

MAR. Friends, today your marriage rites and mine will be celebrated in the presence of the Gods. Eraclea, you have already said that your will is subject to that of Aldimira. Tell me, Aldimira, do you con-

sent for her to be mine?

DEC. (O stars!)

ER. (What will he say?)

DEC. I consent.

ER. I do not.

MAR. Why do you change your mind? You are untrue to yourself, untrue to her, and you are too hostile to my happiness.

ER. Whether I am breaking faith with Aldimira, let her tell you. If it were Aldimira who thus disposes of my will, then I would be faithless to Aldimira.

MAR. What answer do you make? (to DECIO)

DEC. Behold revealed before you the knight who loves her. Behold, I give Eraclea to you. You thought that I was Aldimira, but I am Decio, that Decio who, faithful to Rome, in his native Volturnus was unwilling to stain his steadfast honor, and who now yields his heart to you in Eraclea.

FL.
DAM. }(together) What do I perceive?

IL.
IR. }(together) What do I see?

AL. Unexpected outcome!

MAR. Decio, the Senate of Rome owes you too much, and Marcello is not ungrateful towards your faithfulness. O noble reason, cause the soul to fearlessly exert dominion over the tumult of the senses! Let Decio's faithfulness and Eraclea's love remain happy and glad; and if she is your heart, I give your heart back to you.

DEC. Ah, welcome reward for my faithfulness!

ER. You have given him back his heart, and me my life.

Spofa Irene d'Ilifo.
Dam E Flavia mia .
Er. Veggafi quefto giorno,
    De le mie nozze, e de le voftre adora
Dam. Dolce mio ben .
Fla. Cor mio.
Il. Al fin pur io fon tuo .
Ir. Pur tua fon'io .
Alf E Lilla dove ftà?
Liv. Lilla mi finfi,
    E mi pigliai di te ricreazione.
Alf. O fvergognata mia reputazione .
Mar. A le gioje bel'anime amanti ,
    Che a le gioje v'invita l'amor
Tut. A le gioje bell'anime amanti ,
    Che à le gioje n'invita l'ano
    Quel diletto che nafce da i p a
    E il diletto più dolce d'un co

IL FINE.

IL. Ah, Princess, let Irene be the bride of Iliso.

DAM. And let Flavia be mine.

ER. Let this day be celebrated with my wedding and yours.

DAM. My sweet beloved!

FL. My heart!

IL. Finally I am yours, too.

AL. And where is Lilla?

LI. I pretended to be Lilla and had fun with you.

AL. Ah, my shame and ruined reputation!

MAR. To happiness, fair loving souls, to happiness Love invites you.

ALL To happiness, fair loving souls, to happiness Love invites you. That joy which is born of weeping is the sweetest joy of a heart. To happiness, etc.